Elizabeth's
GARDEN

A journey through grief

ELIZABETH KIDSON

DEDICATION

I dedicate this book to my loving family.
I miss you all so much.
When I left my family behind, I did not realize the cost that I would pay,
I saw the pain my leaving caused as we said our goodbyes. It is easier to
live with my own heartache, than to live with the thought that I caused
heartache to those who love me.

EK VERLANG SO | I MISS YOU SO

Deur die lang, lang nagte | Through the long, long night
bly by my die pynlike gedagte | stays with me are images
aan gesigte vol verdriet | of faces pained
soos uitgekap uit granite | like chiselled granite
of met metal gegiet | or a metallic mold

Dink ek aan die verlede | I think of the past
onthou ek my gebede | and remember my prayers
Dink ek aan die toekoms | I think of the future
is daar al die hoekoms | but find only questions

Dink ek aan vandag | When I think of today
dan is dit my hart wat smag | my heart longs intensely
na alles in die verlede | of all that's in the past
want ek het goeie rede | because I have good reason

Al wat ek jou kan se | All I can say to you
my hart het daar bly le | is that I left my heart behind

Ps 77:4 "You kept my eyes from closing.
I was too troubled to speak.
I thought about the former days, the years of long ago."

CONTENTS

Acknowledgments   ix
Introduction   xi

1. CHILDHOOD   1
   The Whirlwind   2
   Desert Nights   4
   The Sleep Over   6
   Last Snap-Shots   8
   Regrets   10

2. THE BREAKING   13
   Stranger in the Night   14
   Kidnapped   16
   Blyde River Valley   18
   The Breaking   20
   Diapers in the Moonlight   22
   My Little Blue Bottle   24
   My Body Guard   26
   Two Different Worlds   28
   Back Home   30

3. MY HOME BY THE STREAM   33
   The Untraveled Journey   34
   The Stranger Who Stopped   36
   The Early Years   38
   My Home by the Stream   40
   Escalating Violence   42
   Puzzle Pieces   44
   Quiet before the Storm   46
   Unburdened   48

4. LEAVING MY HOMELAND   51
  Far Away   52
  KAALVOET KINDERS   54
  Achille Lauro   56
  Achille Lauro's Tumultuous Past   58
  Empty Walls   60
  Prayer   62
  The Miracle   64
  Bible Roulette   66
  Leaving my Homeland   68

5. DIFFICULT ADJUSTMENTS   71
  Difficult Adjustments   72
  Frankfurt   74
  Car Jacked   76
  Taking Responsibility   78
  The Sliding Scale   80
  Avoidance   82
  Laughter   84
  A Lot to Learn   86
  The Bakery   88
  The Waiting   90
  Mysteries and Paradoxes   92

6. DEATH AND DESTRUCTION   95
  A Lonely Path   96
  Suicide   98
  The Elephant   100
  Emptiness   102
  I Don't Know   104
  My Hiding Place   106
  His Last Wish   108
  God, Why?   110
  Truth   112
  Feeling of Well-Being   114
  Hurricane Andrew   116
  A Tree Planted   118

7. IMMIGRATION   121
   This is the Way   122
   The Visit   124
   Forty-Hour Fast   126
   Our Day in Court   128
   Publix Shooting   130
   Waar is jou Huis dan?   132
   By the Grace of God   134
   South Africa   136
   Grandma Days   138

8. Y2K AND MINDGAMES   141
   Ladies Boot Camp   142
   Change   144
   Bread and Wine   146
   Distance Makes No Difference   148
   Relationships   150
   Total Confusion   152
   The Trading Post   154

9. MY YEAR OF MOURNING   157
   The Question of Faith   158
   Little Did I Know   160
   10/7   162
   Painful Thoughts   164
   Desert Demons   166
   Don't Smoke That Stuff   168
   Heartbreak at Daybreak   170
   The Linking Object   172
   Officer Duncan Kidson Food Pantry   174
   Badge of Hope   176
   All By Myself   178

10. MY TOOLBOX   181
   My Tool Box   182
   Your Brain on Crafting   184
   Stained Glass   188
   Nobody is Promised Tomorrow   190

Forgiveness   192
The Glass Wall   194
Desert Storm   196

11. GRANDMA DAYS   199
Grandkids   200
To Avery   202
Heart Games   204
Locusts   206
Fear of the Unknown   208
Just Being There   210
Where Earth and Heaven Meet   212

Epilogue   215

Timeline   219
About the Author   225

ACKNOWLEDGMENTS

A Family Affair

I never had the self-confidence to write, yet my spirit moved me to create this testimony. I would like to thank my family for being the inspiration for this book.

My daughter Jeanette and her husband Carsten, worked through the many fragmented pieces of my writing. They transformed the skeleton of my vision and fleshed it out with insightful questions which helped me construct my thoughts into meaningful paragraphs.

My daughter Angie spent many hours questioning me about events in my life to ensure I captured all that was needed. She used her amazing talent for writing to bring this book to life.

After months of work my daughter Nita read through the journal and added her own memories to the landscape of this book.

All my daughters experienced life with me and brought their insights to make this a beautifully rounded unification of our recollections.

My therapist Dr. Teddy Tarr was the driving force behind this project. She tirelessly encouraged to publish my testimony and gave me the confidence to do so. She spent many hours reading through my work, making corrections and suggestions and couldn't help but laugh when I told her my daughter Angie wrote my autobiography.

A special thank you to my friend, Sandy Marietta, for the lovely art she created that served as inspiration for the front cover of this book.

INTRODUCTION

Through the years I have often experienced life shattering events, but without fail, almost as if sent by God, someone will show up to support me through the crises and stay as long as needed, sometimes for a few minutes, and other times for years. This is a consistency that flows like a golden thread through my life.

I have written many poems while journaling, I use the dark and painful part of my life, using words to both soothe and understand myself and what is happening. And I keep writing until I have pushed through and reached the light. I would like to tell you my story through the poems that were inspired by my life, along with the versus from the Bible that spoke most directly to me.

I did not plan to write this book, I'd wake up during the night and have a poem on my mind, then felt compelled to write it down immediately. My English was limited at the time and if I had waited until morning, I would have forgotten all but a fragment. Every poem came into being by events I experienced; the words flowed out of me almost as if my heart needed to be heard.

I used the painful experiences of my life that I poured onto paper through the years and turned it into a gift of sorts to you. What started initially as a journal eventually blossomed into this testimony. I began writing as a form of therapy but as the years passed, I realized that the trials and tribulations of my life, and the learning that I received from them, is a gift I can pass on. I made my misfortune work for me, I hope that in reading this, you will not be defeated either.

This is the journey of my life with all the tragic losses, heartbreaking events, bitter moments, and soul-healing laughter. I offer my experiences, my insight, the strength and guidance of my faith, and my thoughts to you. I hope that by sharing my life, others can learn from the mistakes I made and gain a certain wisdom by understanding life as I've experienced it. In these hopes I share my childhood, all the deaths that shadowed my life, the stories of those that I love, and my miraculous experiences with God.

This is not only a story about my journey to a faraway land, but a spiritual journey as well. A story of how my changing beliefs changed my life and brought me to a place I had not hoped existed before.

Jn 14:5 "Lord we don't know where you are going, how can we know the way?" Jesus answered, "I am the way and the truth and the life."

Ps 73:23 "You hold me by my right hand. You guide me with Your counsel."

> *I don't know how to tell my story*
> *because you see....*
> *I don't know how to write*
> *But with God's help I might*
> *finish this book*

then we can look
at what God wants to bring to light
God will send words to write
when the time is right
Imagine my surprise
to see God's power divine
guide my words of love and pain
of all I've lost and gained
The poems tell of the good and bad
but I'll remember all the good I've had

— *GOD KNOWS*

I have put my memories into poems and paragraphs, like building a jigsaw puzzle with poetry. Everyone fits in somewhere, but actually the value is in what lies behind it all. This is my testimony.

Pr 16:9 "In his heart a man plans his course, but the Lord determines his steps."

Chapter One

CHILDHOOD

*All too often the whirlwinds of life will pick me up
and take me where I don't want to go.*

THE WHIRLWIND

Life – always changing, changing
and I am re-arranging
all the many, many pieces
of broken plans and dreams
it takes forever it seems
and life is still changing, changing
whilst I am re-arranging
my broken plans and dreams

LIFE HAPPENS

Ps 139:9 "If I rise on the wings of the dawn; if I settle on the far side of the sea, even there."

Ps 139:10 "Your Hand will guide me. Your right hand will hold me fast."

My earliest childhood memory is about a whirlwind. I was 4-years old when a whirlwind picked up my skinny little body and launched me into a cactus, the result was a thorn in my eye, but that was not the worst part. Being in such distress and pain, I fiercely struggled to free myself from the doctor later that day and fought all who tried to help me. That was a fight not worth winning, when I reflected back on the experience years later, I saw that my struggle to resist help pushed me to wet my pants. It was the whirlwinds of life that picked me up and took me where I didn't want to go. Leaving me in despair and at the mercy of circumstances over which there was no control.

Born and raised in Vryburg, a small town near the Kalahari Desert, I vividly remember oxen pulling large water-wagons through dusty streets only to water a few trees while trying to beat the desert heat. Most of my family lived in the same little town and we visited each other often. On one such a visit when I was 5-years old, my uncle started the prayer before dinner but didn't close his eyes as my dad had taught me to do before prayer. I asked him why did he not close his eyes to which he responded with a question of his own; "do you close your eyes to thank your dad for something?" I replied "no I don't, but my dad is not holy."

As a child, I always had a special awareness of God's presence with me. My younger sister, Lien, and I, usually walked together to church Sunday mornings. At the age of 12, we were greeted one day by a surprise, there was a Christmas tree surrounded by gifts at the church. With great excitement we opened our presents, mine was a beautiful silver broach of two dancing ballerinas, after all these years this piece of jewelry is still a treasured possession.

During my darkest days, it preserved memories of times when life was good, with the feeling of God's love surrounding me. As a teenager, there came a distance between God and myself but each time I held the ballerina broach in my hands, I felt God's presence and love again. As the joy gradually faded out of my life I forgot about my ballerinas, and slowly lost my ability to dance with delight.

DESERT NIGHTS

About a time that was but is no more

It is a cold desert night
with magically bright moonlight
The boy asleep under the wagon
begins to wake with the restless oxen

And black shadows are creeping
towards the boy who was sleeping
Then powerful jaws
grab the blanket made of skin
with the boy wrapped within

A quiver of fear with death so near
The drooling laughing beast
anticipates a feast
but the boy is so brave
and stands up to face
the beast in the night
and puts it to flight

THE HYENA

Dt 32:10 "In a desert land He found him in a barren and howling waste. He shielded him and cared for him."

My dad loved telling stories about his childhood, most especially as we sat around the fire having "braaivleis" (BBQ). He grew up near the Kalahari Desert and described his childhood adventures in the fields with such detail that it transported us into his memories. As teenagers, my dad and his friends transported salt from the mines to the town on ox wagon. The desert nights being so cold, my father would wrap himself in a leather blanket and sleep under the ox wagon, not sleeping much as he would have to defend himself from the hyenas trying to grab his blanket.

Childhood memories, like a treasure chest full of golden nuggets, still enriching my life. My paternal grandmother was a midwife and had a black 'medicine box'. As a child I regarded that mysterious box with great awe and believed the medicine could cure any ailment. Early morning bicycle rides into the fields with my father to pick wildflowers during springtime. Gazing in wonder at the night sky, huge and captivating stars as far as your eye can see, softly lighting up the desert night, creating a serene and fantasy-like scene. My dad and I loved to search for the "Star of David" at Christmas time as we went caroling.

THE SLEEP OVER

My little friend looked so pale and frail
when I stopped by her window that morning
She tried to lift her head to greet
but only our eyes could meet
as I stared at her through the window

That morning she didn't wave to say hello
and somehow, I knew it was her time to go
As I stood by her window later that day
I watched as her little white coffin
was carried away.

— *THE GIRL IN THE*
WINDOW

Isa 60:20,b "The Lord will be your everlasting light, and your days of sorrow will end."

In South Africa the first of September is a special holiday known as 'Lentedag', the first day of spring. There was great excitement in the air, all the girls wore flowers in their hair and white dresses to school, celebrating the beginning of springtime. As a child I had good feelings about school and associated school with the magic to be found in books, I always felt so important with a children's books in hand. That's why my uncle Dawie gave me the nickname "Books."

I was 10-years old when my best friend, Linda, became sick with diphtheria. In the mornings, on my way to school, I would stop at her house gate which was marked with yellow flags to indicate quarantine. She would sit up and wave at me through her window, but as time went by, she struggled to wave back. Shortly thereafter her little white coffin was carried away and the yellow flags removed. Her loss left me longing for my best friend and left me feeling misunderstood and alone.

Although I enjoyed school and had a supportive family, there were many difficulties during my school years. What I did, or didn't do, often turned out wrong even though it was not done deliberately. In spite of seldom being the teacher's pet, I really liked school as a young child. But timidity made me an easy target to be picked on and gradually a belief began to develop that life would always bring disappointments. Repetitive, unpleasant experiences enforced this negative thinking as I grew.

The first and last time I had a sleep-over at a friend's home, I experienced a scary and disturbing scene. Late that night my friend's intoxicated father began to beat his wife and children, leaving the mother's face covered in blood. Fearing for our safety, we ran and hid in the garden while the father searched for us. Fortunately, a car stopped in the street and shaking with fear, we ran to the car and begged the driver to take us to the police station. I have no recollection what happened at the police station or how we got home from there.

LAST SNAP-SHOTS

Every deed is a seed
planted to grow
for all time
Take heed of the seed
and plant what you need
to let goodness aglow

— *THE SEED*

Isa 30:18 "Yet the Lord longs to be gracious to you; He rises to show you compassion."

My mom was a seamstress in her younger years, she made my dresses, knit my sweaters, and also taught me to sew and knit. She was in poor health most of her life and almost died as a baby. My grandparents bought a grandfather clock so that the hourly chimes could serve as reminders to give my mother her medicine timeously. I now have this precious clock which was made in Germany in the 1920's. My grandfather died when my mom was a young girl, leaving my grandmother to take care of eight children. As a substitute teacher at the local farm school, she didn't have much income. What was most impressive about grandma was her ornate, flowing handwriting, unforgettably beautiful.

I was 13-years old when we moved from Vryburg, to Pretoria, a large city and completely different to what we had known. My youngest sister, Annelize who was 3 at the time, had cerebral palsy and needed to go to a special school. My brother Boeta was 5-years old and wouldn't walk due to a painful problem with his hips and so we made the move to accommodate those needs. Boeta spent one year in an orthopedic hospital for treatment, missing his first year of school. With the result that afterwards, he never really blended into life outside the hospital walls. It was also a difficult adjustment and not a very successful one for me; it was much harder to cope in school; my nice picture books turned into complicated textbooks and lost their magic. The fact that we often moved during my high school years made it more difficult to keep up. Annelize, on the other hand, made great progress and enjoyed the school routine tremendously, but tragically 2-years later she died unexpectedly in her sleep.

It was the day before my fifteenth birthday, awoken by my mother screaming as she held the lifeless body of my 5-year-old sister. My little sister, who shared a bedroom with me, died in her sleep when her lungs failed. Oblivious to the life and death struggle that occurred just a few feet from me, I hadn't woken up. To this day, I remember the lividity on my sister's cheek, the bruise that settled in after she passed. In spite of the make-up the mortuary applied, this mark was still visible at her viewing. These last snapshots had always been very traumatic to me and tried hard not to revisit them in my mind.

It is now decades later and I'm still traumatized by those events, fearing history may repeat itself and I will wake up one morning to find my husband is no longer with me.

REGRETS

Today is play day. Tomorrow is pay day

> *You will get burned*
> *when you play with fire*
> *and that's not God's desire*
> *but even so*
> *He will not go*
> *He will be with you*
> *all the way*
> *till you can see it through*
> *and choose the wiser way*
>
> *PLAYING WITH*
> *FIRE*

Mt 28:20 "And surely, I am with you always, till the very end of the age."

My cousin Henning lived with us during the time of my sister's death. We were best friends and didn't make it easy for my parents. This was a particularly difficult time for my mother, yet at the time I shared little empathy for her. I was dating someone against my parent's wishes and didn't want to listen to their point of view. They tried everything possible to discourage the relationship, even resorting to packing up the family and moving to another town, but I was blind and deaf to their pleas. After Annelize died, my parents didn't want to fight me anymore.

As a child, I was never the victim of bad situations in my home, but as a teenager became the victim of my own bad choices. I didn't understand that life does not revolve around me. There is a bigger picture and that's where everything that effects life begins. My decisions during my teenage years had a traumatic impact on my life and hurt many people who cared deeply about me. At that time, unfortunately, I was too immature to deny my selfish desires and failed to see the hardships following the path of my choices. Even though my past cannot be fixed or changed, I do not forget the cost of my errors and remember well the lessons it bought me.

I was in an abusive relationship and did not have the emotional strength to break free, or even to recognize how damaging it was, I had come to believe that I was nothing without the relationship. I eventually married him, and the negative consequences of that choice came back a hundred-fold. Being physically beaten before we got married, there is no excuse that I didn't know what I was in for, even now I struggle to think back to what made me marry him.

As a young person I made promises in good faith, but when reality set in, my perception changed, and I could no longer be true to what I had promised.

Chapter Two

THE BREAKING

Reality accepts no excuses.

STRANGER IN THE NIGHT

My grandmother used to say: "You cannot reason with an angry man."

Affection is like flowers
Beautifully delicate
but will eventually fade away
if not treasured every day
and gets trampled under feet
like dirt in the street.

— *AFFECTION*

Isa 59:1 "Surely the arm of the Lord is not too short to save, nor His ear too dull to hear, but your iniquities have separated you from your God."

I was eight months pregnant with my son Mick, when late one night we were on our way to my parents' home where we lived at the time. Suddenly the car stalled and wouldn't start again, in a fit of anger, brought on by frustration, my husband grabbed me by my hair and viciously slammed my head onto the steering wheel.

Then like a whirlwind sent from the angels, a man appeared by my window, asking me if I am okay. Startled, my husband let go off my hair, turned the key in the ignition and the car started. I never answered that kind stranger but saw him standing there in the dark, watching, as we drove away.

As the months went by it became clear to me that my husband was not going to change. In the beginning of our relationship, I ignored a crucial law; I didn't put ground rules in place of what was acceptable behavior and what wasn't. I didn't realize what should be tolerated when we first met, and that mistake set how we interacted through the years to come. We teach others how to treat us by our own behavior, this is some good old-time wisdom. It's very unlikely that bad behavior is going to get better, but it is very likely it will escalate. My son, Mick, was nine months old and I was pregnant with my daughter, Nita, when I decided to leave my husband.

My parents moved quite a distance away, to Waterval-Boven, a picturesque little town in the mountains and I looked forward to spending this time with them. My dad and I loved to go trout fishing even though we never caught anything, the peace of the river, the sound of the water and the chirping of birds, restored my heart. I needed this time of peace and tranquility to regain my strength and recover emotionally.

KIDNAPPED

Reality accepts no excuses

It is easy to say
I do or I don't
but I can't really tell
till reality sets in
Only then will I know
if I will or I won't

REALITY

Ro 7:15 "I do not understand what I do. For what I want to do I do not do, but what I hate I do."

I spent a wonderful time with my parents, feeling more optimistic about the future with each passing day. Unfortunately, this relaxing time came abruptly to an end much sooner than I would have liked. After only a few weeks with my parents, my husband and his father arrived unannounced. They insisted that I return with them and when I refused, they suddenly took Mick, my 9-month-old son, got into their car and drove back to Pretoria. They left without diapers, a change of clothes, or his bottle.

I was devastated and inconsolable and first thing the next morning, my dad and I went to court but were told that nothing could be done while we were still married. Later that same day my husband came back, alone. He told me Mick was crying all the time and wouldn't eat or sleep and that he had come to get me. My dad is a very gentle man but that day he was ready to take out his whip. I had never seen him that angry in my life.

I had a complicated pregnancy, and the five-hour car trip back to Pretoria concerned my parents a great deal, but I felt there was no choice and left with my husband to be with Mick. He was so glad to see me but I was too exhausted and weak to do anything and was of no help at all. My husband got very frustrated with me responded by slapping and kicking me to the floor, it was more than my fragile body could endure. The next day I felt even worse. I left Mick with his grandparents and went to the bus stop to get to a doctor but became unconscious from loss of blood.

Bystanders called from the convenience store for an ambulance that arrived within minutes. The hospital was just a few blocks away and the paramedics got me there quickly. Shortly afterwards I received a blood transfusion but had to stay in hospital for a while and on bed rest for the remainder of my pregnancy. My parents came to visit me in hospital and took Mick back with them as I was unable to take care of him.

BLYDE RIVER VALLEY

The day I left my baby
I thought one day maybe
we will have a home
then I won't be alone

I learned to cope
as I found new hope
now I can joyfully sing
as a new life begins
and I can be with my son
in the days to come

— *MY SON*

Ps 77:1 "I cried out to God for help; I cried out to God to hear me. When I was in distress, I sought the Lord."

I was not ready to give up on my marriage yet. Our move to the Blyde River Valley was another hopeful effort to try and make our relationship work. The word "Bly" means happy. This valley, breathtaking in its splendor, with mountains, waterfalls, and rivers, is like a little lost piece of paradise. This was where my mind was at peace and my soul found rest.

My daughter, Nita, was born in the neighboring town, Sabie, while we lived there. My husband quickly found work and for a time, things looked promising. But after being there for a few months we were back to square one. For no discernable reason he left his job, our house, the furniture, everything, and went back to his parents.

We moved to this valley of happiness in the pursuit thereof but found none. This caused me to lose all hope in having a better future, all my great expectations came to nothing. It wrecked me to accept the fact that we had to move from this peaceful valley, so dear to me, and see in ruins the optimistic plans that brought us there. Most of our personal belongings had to be left behind, it was so difficult to close the door and walk away.

There really was no other choice but to go back home to my parents. My daughter was a few months old when I left her and her brother with my parents as there were no opportunities to earn a living in such a small town. Moving back to Pretoria was the only way to find work so I could support myself and my children. It took a while to find employment and a room to rent before my children could come and live with me.

THE BREAKING

As the novelty wears off, the shoe starts to hurt

Eventually, after many months and difficult obstacles to overcome, all my plans came together and my two children, Mick and Nita, returned to live with me. Unfortunately, I married a man who was incapable of carrying the responsibility of a job, a home, and a family. He lived with his parents while I was left tending to the kids alone with no financial support.

One Saturday morning, I left my children with a neighbor to do my weekly shopping. The store was a few blocks away and soon I was on my way back with a heavy bag under each arm. Then, almost home, the unthinkable happened, the bags tore and my groceries dropped to the ground, my desperate effort to catch them all was fruitless.

Standing just across the street from home, everything was scattered at my feet. In the same manner, my life was also torn apart with little that could be done, being so close, yet so far away, I kept watching the house in the hope that someone would come and help me. But the longer I waited the more I realized that I had to go and fetch containers. I was hesitant to leave as I had no money left to buy more food after the nursery school, rent, and bus fare were paid. Fortunately, everything was still there by the time I made it back with the containers.

The torn bags with groceries scattered at my feet, represented my life in different ways. While trying my utmost to keep it together, the bags kept on tearing and valuable contents kept dropping to the ground. In reality there was no point in staying it would only prolong the inevitable. That day my journey in life began. It took courage to let go of the familiar and reach out to the unfamiliar, to have a better life, and to leave the place where I was. Fear to reach out to the unknown shouldn't stop me from making the necessary changes. Sadly, it couldn't be done without breaking out of my dysfunctional marriage so I could start moving towards a life with stability.

> *My life and times are in Your hands*
> *There is no-one who better understands*
> *my dreams, my hopes, and my agony*
> *Dear Lord, you are my destiny*
>
> *MY DESTINY*

Ps 31:14 "But I trust in You, O Lord; my times are in Your hands."

DIAPERS IN THE MOONLIGHT

Why me, why me?
what could God possibly see
in someone like me

I say it because I know
the wrong places I quickly go
but the good I do, oh, so slow

God already sees the me
that I will one day be
Jesus bought me, I am free

YES ME

Pr 3:5 "Trust in the Lord with all your heart and lean not on your own understanding; in all your ways acknowledge Him and He will make your paths straight."

This was a very difficult time for me, emotionally and physically, tending to my children alone was no easy task. In the evenings, after getting home from work, I did the washing by hand and hung it on the line to dry. After dinner, my kids were bathed in a little baby bath, then in the same water, I would soak the dirty clothes to wash the next evening.

My neighbor, Kallie, kindheartedly joked about my diapers in the moonlight. One evening, coming home from work, all my clothes were missing from the line. I panicked until Kallie approached with everything nicely folded. After that day, he did my laundry by hand and hung it on the line while I fed and bathed the kids.

Those early mornings were unbearable waking with exhaustion, leaving late, with a baby on each hip, I had to run to catch the bus. During those days I didn't think better times would ever come or even dreamed about driving my own car one day. It seemed as if life couldn't get any worse, but then it did.

My children were back with me for only a short while before Mick become very sick, he had jaundice and spent two weeks in hospital. After his release, he was home in bed for another week. By losing so much time from work and also paying 20% of all the medical bills, it became financially impossible to continue. All my efforts were not enough to make it on my own. There was no help from their father so eventually my children had to return to my parents. It broke my heart, but there was nothing else left for me to do.

MY LITTLE BLUE BOTTLE

A red light along the way
means stop or you will pay
God who cares for us so much
also warns and keeps in touch

With patience He teaches and guides
when we will stay by His side
If we will listen to His voice
He will show us the better choice

— *WARNINGS*

Ps 41:2 "The Lord will protect him and preserve his life."

As a young girl of 17, my aunt Rika gave me a small dark blue bottle of perfume, with a fragrance so delightful, nothing else could compare. With great disappointment came the realization that the bottle was almost empty. Then by making the unfortunate decision to add a few drops of water to the perfume, I lost it all and ended up with a worthless, watered-down version of my lovely perfume. Sadly, my relationship with God was also being watered down to something so insignificant, I couldn't even recognize Christ's presence with me during my darkest days.

I have distanced myself from God and for a long time was not on friendly terms with Him. I began to suffer guilt that grew steadily and wanted to die but was too afraid to take my own life. Death itself did not scare me but going to hell did.

That fear most likely saved my life. But the pain overwhelmed me, and heartache rooted deep within, like an earthquake, it shook me from my core and I shattered. There were many days I just sat and cried with little interest in life, losing a lot of weight, at 5.6 feet I weighed about 85 pounds at my lowest point.

Feelings of pending doom, an unidentified danger which was very scary to deal with, threatened me. How can something be dealt with when you don't know where the danger hides? Desperately trying to get away but not knowing where to run to. Feeling totally helpless because of my lack of understanding of what to do next, left me with great frustration. I saw myself as a worthless failure with no hope for the future.

During this time, getting more and more confused about what was reality, a bad dream, or a frightening hallucination, one night I 'saw' two black horses running bewildered in a thunderstorm, pulling a chariot. There was a naked body in the chariot, covered with blood, the horses were running wild, the wind was howling, blowing fiercely with thunder and lightning that lit up the dark night. As lightning struck, wind blew the hair away and uncovered the face of the body, and I saw that the face was mine.

MY BODY GUARD

Bad is like a boomerang, if I throw it out there, it will come right back at me.

It was impossible to function with all these negative feelings and awful thoughts. I bit the inside of my mouth until it was bleeding to try and stop these hostile thoughts against God, but these uncontrollable thoughts had a life of their own and went wherever they wanted until it all became too much to bear. After a breakdown, I was admitted into a psychiatric ward at the Astrid Clinic. Through all my misery, God never abandoned me, but I failed to see that He always carried me through darkness and at the clinic God sent a Christian psychiatrist to support me.

Dr. Vivier helped me understand all the factors that were controlling me and brought me to this point in my life. He helped me to pick up the pieces of my shattered self and put them back together again. Concerning my marriage, Dr. Vivier told me the clay I chose to work with was too brittle, and all my efforts to create something from it would have broken regardless. He said if there was a light in the tunnel, he would help me to get there. After being in Dr. Vivier's care for a while, and with his support, I started the divorce proceedings.

After the paperwork for a divorce was filed, my soon to be ex-spouse made my life unbearable and a mutual friend had to introduce me to a man who became my 'bodyguard.' Out of the goodness of his heart, he took it upon himself to watch over me until the divorce was finalized and it was time for me to move back home to my parents and children.

On misty days
as I look through the haze
time seems covered in forgetfulness
and reality in gentleness
Life forgets to be cruel today
and reality chooses the gentler way

Surroundings covered softly
on misty days
and as a new life with God begins
I can feel His presence gently
like the mist upon my skin

— *MISTY DAYS*

Isa 50:2 "When I came, why was there no-one? When I called why was there no-one to answer? Was My arm too short to ransom you?"

TWO DIFFERENT WORLDS

Relationships are a lot like new shoes, if it is not a good fit, they will only bring pain and discomfort. It is better to leave them on the shelf no matter how good they look. Don't think they will become comfortable after a while, it's not going to happen, so from the very start it is best to just steer clear.

I didn't really know him
and he didn't really know me
We lived in two different worlds
without much common ground

I was in the trenches – every day
fighting to find a better way
to master this disaster

And so we continued
to live our separate lives
even though there was a bridge
because he wouldn't cross that
and I couldn't…

— THE BRIDGE

2 Co 6:14 "Do not be yoked together with unbelievers. For what do right-eousness and wickedness have in common? Or what fellowship can light have with darkness? What does a believer have in common with an unbeliever?"

.   .   .

Everything the Bible warns us against is not to spoil our fun but to protect us from harm. As a child I had a great awareness of God's presence with me, but as a teenager, unfortunately, I chose the company of non-believers and drifted away from my Christian faith and principles.

I married a man who took no responsibility to help provide a home for his family, or to help take care of them. I had been trying to build on sand from the beginning, but it collapsed every time. Without that firm foundation to rely on, there was nothing left to work with and no possibility for a reconciliation. I was left without any help, but God came to my rescue and sent people to support and care for me during these trying times. Now I have a new and much deeper understanding about the seriousness of the warnings from the Bible.

1 Jn 2:15 "Do not love the world or anything in the world. If anyone loves the world the love of the Father is not in him. (17) The world and its desires pass away, but the man who does the will of God lives forever."

BACK HOME

I had a lot of baggage full of garbage

A sure way to fail is to jump into life recklessly without a plan or thought. I turned away from God, took a walk on the wild side and came back to Him bruised and beaten, barely escaping with my life. Things didn't fall apart overnight however, there were many choices and circumstances that led me there, and a destructive thought process paved the way. It was a slow breaking down process, a deterioration of my mind, and similarly, my recovery will also be a slow building-up process.

Now, really knowing Jesus, it was difficult for me to understand that He will take me as a failure and make a success out of me. An important lesson for me to learn was that the way I saw myself is the way I could be. God changed my negative thoughts into positive ones and gave to me a life that honors Him. I am His beloved; He will say to me: *(Isa 43:4) "You are precious and honored in My sight because I love you." (Isa 9:6) He will be called Wonderful Counselor, Mighty God, Everlasting Father, Prince of peace*

> *The Prince of peace came to me*
> *and taught me how to be*
> *happy, joyful and free*
> *grateful for the future I see*

I don't find it confusing to think about God as one and also three; the Father, the Son, and the Holy Spirit. I have a body, a soul, and a spirit and all three honor Him. At times I am in such awe with the presence of God I feel almost overwhelmed by his majesty, I will kneel down in prayer and feel Jesus' presence with me, then I'll lean against Him and pour out my heart and share all my feelings of sorrow and disappointment, feelings so raw it cannot be put into words. I imagine He puts His hand upon my head, telling me that everything is going to be okay.

I have pictures in my mind
of God – so gentle and kind
with thoughts too tender to say
I have only feelings to pray

The God of the heavenly lights
brightens up my darkest nights
with my burden, how heavy it may be
Oh Lord, I trust only in Thee

— *I TRUST IN THEE*

Ps 55:17 "Evening, morning, and noon, I cry out in distress and He hears my voice."

Chapter Three

MY HOME BY THE STREAM

Even though I cannot remember, I cannot forget either.

THE UNTRAVELED JOURNEY

Him of whom I am so fond
the treasures of his mind
lies deep like a bottomless pond
and will take a lifetime to find
Him whom I love so well
Forever together we will dwell

— HIM, WHOM I
LOVE

Mk 10:7 "For this reason a man will leave his father and mother and be united to his wife and the two will become one flesh."

My paternal grandmother died in June of 1972, shortly after I moved back to my parent's home. The funeral brought many people to our home and it was there that I met the man of my dreams. In the hallway by the front door was a linen chest, I was searching through it for guest towels when a young man came through the door behind me. It was love at first sight for both of us and we married a year later. It was a marvelous blessing after a period of so much pain, but it brought with it sorrow of its own. We were devastated with the loss of our first baby.

The birth pains were real but way too soon
Too soon his life came to an end
Hours and minutes twist and turn

lost in endlessness
Emptiness reached out into nothingness
Hands stretched out trusting
just to withdraw with nothing
but the emptiness
As I feel the whole of me
shake and break and fall apart
and with it ends my peace of mind
my will to mend

— *A MOMENT FOR BABY*
JACOB

Ps 30:11 "You turned my wailing into dancing; You removed my sack-cloth and clothed me with joy that my heart may sing to You and not be silent."

How can one know the way of an untraveled journey? It was impossible to grasp the depth of pain a stillborn baby brings when my cousin Henning and his wife lost their baby, but now I am all too familiar with that pain. One day I was dressed in maternity clothes, the next, in sackcloth. Nobody bonded with the baby, except his parents, and so our grief was ours alone to bare. The doctor told me the baby was badly deformed and my body had rejected him, still that didn't make my acceptance of the loss any easier. Yet 18-months later God blessed us with twin boys, Laurence and Duncan, and all the sadness changed into crazy activity.

THE STRANGER WHO STOPPED

In the early years of our marriage, we moved around quite a bit. During one of these moves, while packing up, I removed the safety locks from the cabinet doors in the bathroom. When the moving company arrived, I let them in and showed them where to start packing. Unbeknownst to me my 18-month-old twin boys got into the bathroom cabinet and managed to open a bottle of prescription strength pain pills. Later, I found the boys on the bathroom floor with pills in their mouths and the bottle almost empty.

Early the morning I was ready to begin
While busy packing – I let the movers in
after they knocked on the door
a while later, going back to the bathroom
I found my twin boys on the floor
In their hands, a half empty bottle of pills
They just looked so pale and so still
Panicked, I left the movers standing there
the twins needed urgent medical care
Without a moment's hesitation
I grabbed them and in desperation
put them in their stroller and ran
to the preachers house fast as I can
and banged on the door but nobody's home
I felt so afraid and desperately alone
when a car came down the street
and the stranger realized my need
He stopped and got out
I ran to him for help, begged and shout
as we got the boys in his car
and raced to a hospital not that far –

just a few miles away
To the stranger who stopped that day
I am forever grateful
a man I never saw again but will always remember
Thank you

— *MOVING DAY*

Ps 22:11 "Do not be far from me, for trouble is near and there is no-one to help."

A stranger who happened to be close helped me to the hospital with my twins. I stayed there all day until late that night while the doctor pumped their stomachs and gave them medicine through intravenous drips, which had to be inserted into their heads due to their age. I forgot all about the movers and the stroller left on the street corner, while the hospital notified my husband, who went home to take care of the move and recover the stroller. The next day, thanks to God, the stranger who stopped, and the medical staff, my boys were back to their normal mischievous selves.

ELIZABETH KIDSON

THE EARLY YEARS

I had my hands full with the twin boys and not only wished for but needed extra hands! 2.4-years after their birth, my husband and I were blessed again with the addition of our twin girls, Angela and Jeanette.

The excitement of having two twins was unbelievable, but it was an impossible task to keep up with them all, most especially the boys. During nap time I'd put them in their bedroom and close the door where they usually fell asleep with ease. When the twin girls were 11-months old and the twin boys were 3-years old, I found their bedroom door open and their beds empty. Leaving the twin girls in the house I frantically searched for the boys and eventually found them a block away from the house on their way to "somewhere". When their adventures happened more than once we had to investigate how they managed to leave their bedroom, never mind the house, as they were too short to reach the door handle.

My plan was executed one day when, after I put them in their room for nap time and closed the door, I went outside to watch them through the window. I was astonished to see that they worked together to take their little mattress off their bed and them to the door. Lawrence would stand on the mattress and hang on the door handle while Duncan pulled the mattress out from under him. Still clinging to the handle, Lawrence swung open the door and out they went, showing remarkable communication and teamwork for their young age. These two little escape artists had to be watched all the time.

As a child we had a tin full of seashells and it was my own special magic to rest the seashell against my ear and listen to the soothing sound of the ocean. Years later we were thrilled with the opportunity to live by the sea. We moved to Amanzimtoti when the twin girls were 2-years old, and the twin boys were 4-years old. While unpacking boxes, we became aware that Laurence and Duncan were missing once again and began our frantic search by running up and down the street calling out for them. After a while of fruitless searching, I finally saw them sitting on the pavement under a tree accompanied by a bottle of peppermint liquor which they tried to open. To my question as to where they got it from, Duncan told me they went into the neighbor's house and took it from the cabinet.

The twin boys would continue to test us with their abilities to evade and explore for many years, not until they went to primary school did their temperaments moderate.

It was a real team effort to travel with the four little ones. My oldest son Mick, and my oldest daughter Nita, my husband, and myself were each responsible for one of the children. Our system worked well when the two sets of twins ran off in four different directions, making the chase a lot easier for one tired adult. It would have been impossible to keep up with the twins without Mick and Nita's help. After the twin girls were born, Mick got up at night to care for the twin boys, he was already such a considerate child, even at the tender age of 10-years old. When he was older, he would offer to make breakfast in the mornings and get his five siblings ready for school. He continued supporting the large family this way until he graduated from high school, when he left for the army for two years compulsory military service.

Pr 22:6 "Train a child in the way he should go and when he is old, he will not turn from it."

MY HOME BY THE STREAM

It's nice to dream
about a home by the stream
where monkeys play
early in the day

Too much to ask I would say
but God gave it anyway
A beautiful valley and peace
with years to stay but then to leave.

GOD GIVES

Ps 23:2 "He makes me lie down in green pastures, He leads beside quiet water, He restores my soul."

It was with great excitement that we moved to Queensburgh, Durban in the beginning of January 1980. Our beautiful new home in the mountains was more like a vacation home. We had a spectacular garden with mango, pawpaw, banana trees and mulberry trees growing in abundance. Our property sloped down to the river and early in the mornings mist would settle on the mountains and little monkeys played in the trees. When we sat outside, the sound of water babbling over the rocks and the birds singing completed the picture. Life was good.

A little downstream from us was a deep pool, a perfect place to swim and lie on the large rocks as we basked in the sun. Upstream was a dense overgrowth of wild bananas, ferns and palms just before you reached a clearing. Just beyond that, almost by surprise, was an idyllic holiday resort in all its splendor. Down the street from us was a family who kept beautiful horses, who were tame and gentle. My children, who had no experience horseback riding, weren't intimidated at all and were always welcome to go for rides. This was so much more than a house in a great neighborhood, it had a mystical element, a trifecta of God, love, and life combined in perfect proportions.

We shared many happy times in that house, it was some of the best years of our lives. Needless to say, the kids got into quite a bit of mischief and between them all, it was never easy to find the guilty party. The plan was to send all four of the younger children to their bedroom to contemplate their actions. When they remembered who the guilty one was, they could come and talk to us. One afternoon, while preparing dinner, a stranger stormed into my kitchen. Furiously, she told me that she had almost killed two of my children. I called the kids so I could address the guilty parties. The lady went from furious, to shocked, and then confused as my two sets of identical twins ran into the kitchen. Momentarily speechless, she frustratingly explained that one boy rode a bike with a girl on the handlebars and she almost ran them over as they pulled in front of her while she turned a corner in her car. Unable to pinpoint which of the four children were the culprits, she left in total disbelief with nothing else to say to me.

Unfortunately, this idyllic time in our lives was also a time of escalating violence. The emotional end of Apartheid was escalating with bombs going off frequently in public places with horrific results, shattering our peaceful existence.

ESCALATING VIOLENCE

There's darkness all around me
and then came thunder clouds
I tried so hard but could not see
So, I cried out loud

I'm in trouble with nothing left
They say God is just a prayer away
But I don't know what to say
Lord, please teach me how to pray

— DARK DAYS

Isa 59:9 "So justice is far from us, and righteousness does not reach us. We look for light, but all is darkness, for brightness, but we walk in deep shadows."

We lived during a time of escalating violence that touched every walk of life. Bombs went off regularly in public places with tragic results. One Christmas Eve, as Santa handed out gifts from underneath a Christmas tree at the local mall, a bomb went off in the middle of the crowd. Instant chaos and panic surrounded the shoppers, mingled together with blood and torn bodies. When the firefighters arrived, they used their hose pipes to not only put out the fire, but to clean the blood stains.

Going to the mall during those times was like the airports of today, having to pass through metal detectors and being searched by security. There were police with their dogs patrolling the mall during business hours, making grocery shopping a nerve wrecking experience. No more leisurely walks through the mall over weekends indulging in window-shopping, or meeting friends for coffee. These times became increasingly stressful and complicated, school children were taught what to do in case of an attack and did regular 'bomb drills' and practiced safety procedures, learning about secure places to hide in case of an attack. With regular threats targeting schools, this was a real threat and many parents were hesitant to send their children to school.

This was the time my eldest son, Mick, came of age. He was preparing for his 2-year mandatory military service when my maternal grandmother had a fatal heart attack. Grieved and heartbroken, I had to miss her funeral in order to send my son to war. Mick asked our friend, Dessie, to pray, because he didn't want me to cry while I took him to the drop-off point. The army officials assured the parents that everything would be done to secure the boys' safety, but they would encounter conflict and, unfortunately, not all of them would return from the border. I kept my tears hidden until I got home, then sobbed uncontrollably.

While praying for my son, a mental image came to mind of a leopard in a tree and a Sheppard with a lamb on His shoulders. I knew that although my son would be in dangerous situations, God would protect him and bring him home safe. During Mick's second year of military service, he suffered severe burns on his legs. He was hospitalized and after his recovery, continued serving his time at the hospital, completing his two-year mandatory service.

PUZZLE PIECES

I believe in Christianity as I believe that the sun has risen, not because I see it, but because by it I see everything.

—*CS Lewis*

When I have a problem and I pray
I'll record what God has to say
I will write the answer down
and don't care when people frown

When it happens, all will know
that God said so, some time ago
My children see the special way
how God still speaks to us today

— *TAKE TIME TO*
LISTEN

Dt 11:19 "Teach them to your children, talking about them when you sit at home. Write them on the doorframes of your houses and on your gates."

We went to a conservative church for many years, my spiritual life at the time was not much to get excited about. I tried to read the Bible but couldn't relate to most of it. It was like having a bag full of jig-saw puzzle pieces thrown on the ground without a picture to guide me. Perhaps the puzzle box was lost in the Garden of Eden when man traded innocence for the knowledge of good and evil. For me, Bible study is when God, like a parent, sits with His child and helps to find the right pieces, one piece at a time. The more time we spend with God in Bible study, the more pieces come together, the clearer the picture becomes, and the better we can understand the design.

Church service teaches religion and theories but cannot teach faith in God. An old family friend, Dessie, came to the rescue while I was struggling during that time. He was in Bible College and shared the study material that they covered each week with me. God taught me amazing lessons through these studies, little by little an understanding began to develop of God's message to me. It was the beginning of a complete change in my journey as a Christian. God became a very real presence in my life and for the first time I could say: "I love You Lord" and truly mean it.

Christianity is a *relationship* with God as my Father, and my trust in God developed and continues to strengthen through years of personal experience. Listening to Him, timely words illuminate my thoughts and put situations in perspective. I use the poems in my journal to build my jigsaw puzzle, even though the big picture is still unknown to me. God instructs me, leads me, and protects me, but it is impossible to fully comprehend the vastness of God's Word. One day I will see the picture on the box and then I will know.

1 Co 13:12 "Now we see but a poor reflection as in a mirror; then we shall see face to face. Now I know in part; then I shall know fully."

QUIET BEFORE THE STORM

Growing up near the Kalahari Desert, I am familiar with the harsh ways, the emptiness, the nothingness, of the dessert. As a young person, the desert was not a pleasant place for me to be in, but later in life I realized I belong there. It revived an understanding of where my roots were and where my place should be. Becoming more and more aware of God's presence in my life, my outlook started to change. At the right time a meaningful picture of the purpose God intended for me, will be revealed. It's in this desert place of nothingness and emptiness where God can meet me and teach me.

Prayer is not just an act of doing, but more about *being*. God will speak to me when I'm quiet and able to listen. When I first met my husband, he was on my mind just about every waking hour; first thing in the morning and the last thought at night. Similarly, continuous feelings of adoration towards God is the most beautiful form of prayer one can think of. I believe that is what the apostle Paul meant when he said we should pray all day long, it is not just the words, but an expression of my devotion.

From time-to-time God will answer my prayer in a dream, or with a message from the Bible, and at other times with an image in my thoughts. One New Year's Eve while praying, as I was asking God's blessing on the coming year, there was a picture in my mind of a beautiful misty valley, and like the mist, the peace of God was all around and encircled me. It is impossible to convey this experience. The rest of that year was lovely and peaceful, yet it was the quiet year before the stormy ones.

I tell you my story
of all God's glory

and the answers He reveals
with an image in my thoughts
or a message in my dreams

I see every day
how God still conveys
with His children this way
so they can say to everyone…
"This is what the Lord has done…"

— *VISIONS*

Nu 12:6 (b) "I reveal Myself to him in visions, I speak to him in dreams."

Da 2:19 "During the night the mystery was revealed to Daniel in a vision then Daniel praised the God of heaven."

UNBURDENED

Even though I could not remember, I could not forget either

> *There is such peace to find*
> *when I can open my mind*
> *and let God unburden my thoughts*
> *Then I can spend the night*
> *as I lay down my head*
> *and drifts off to sleep –*
> *in God's perfect rest*

— *IF I CAN*

Mt 11:28 "Come to Me, all you who are weary and burdened and I will give you rest."

I have always been afraid of the water but never understood why, then came the day when it was time to face my fear and learn how to swim. Duncan bought me an orange life vest and encouraged me to get my feet wet. So, there I was, standing in 4-feet of water wearing my over-sized life vest, clinging to the side of the pool. But the life vest had to be taken off before I could learn to swim. My first lesson taught me more than how to swim, it triggered a childhood memory. Soon after that I began having nightmares.

As a young child I witnessed the drowning of my uncle's friend, Tom. We were picnicking when Tom decided to swim across the dam. Halfway across his legs began to cramp and he couldn't make it back to land. Later, his body was found between the reeds, and he was carried past me after they recovered his body. An image of his face, the red hair, freckles, and his blue lips remained in my sub-conscious. Loss can dwell with us all our lives, this traumatic experience remained with me all these years and hugely impacted my life. Even though I could not remember, I could not forget either.

Another childhood memory that burdened my mind was betrayal. I was 8-years old and playing at our neighbor's house and a little girl who lived on a nearby farm played with us. We had a dog who would playfully chase after us when we ran away. This little girl was afraid of the dog and ran into a bedroom, shutting the door. I knocked and asked her to let me in but didn't tell her that the dog was with me, when she opened the door, the dog charged inside. She panicked when she saw him and jumped onto the bed screaming, and then the dog bit her.

The adults quickly came to her side, I was still in shock and couldn't move, it was if my brain had stopped recording. I couldn't remember the attack or recall any of the details until one day while praying, it all came flooding back. That little girl trusted me, and I had betrayed her trust by not telling her the dog was with me. I asked God to help her to forgive me and to heal her if she was traumatized. I am so very sorry that this happened.

Chapter Four

LEAVING MY HOMELAND

Gone are all those familiar roads that lead to familiar places.

FAR AWAY

Today I feel so sad
I really miss my mom and dad
They are so far away
If only they could come to stay

They have silver hair and hearts of gold
All the things they have told
are precious and will hold
their value, even when I'm old

MOM AND DAD

My mom never complained about all the sacrifices she made for us; she was there every day to meet me as I got home from school. Walking into the kitchen, the smell of dinner on the stove gave me that "coming home" feeling of contentment. My mother suffered with kidney trouble and was in poor health most of her life. There were times I could see in her eyes that she was feeling ill, but dinner was always ready for us all. Living a sheltered life as I grew, I didn't grasp at the time how much my mom meant to me, but later, and after being exposed to the harsher realities of life, I developed a deep appreciation for my mother and everything she did for me.

My mom was like an oasis in the desert, a place I could rest when life was harsh and unforgiving. She helped me moving forward when I was too tired to continue, she was a blessing in every sense.

As a young man my dad began his career with the Railways, and later fulfilled his dream to become a teacher, where he taught at Enslin Park Railway College. After his retirement, my parents moved back to the Vryburg area, near the Kalahari Desert, and bought a small farm where they had a few animals, fruit and vegetable crops, and a spectacular rose garden. The soil was unforgiving though, and it rarely rained. With great expectation my dad would watch the clouds and exclaimed: "Die wolkies lyk belowend vandag." which means "the clouds are promising rain today". Desert people appreciate rain greatly for the life it brings.

My parents gave me many gold nuggets they found, I still have them and treasure them for their memories. I was 11-years old when I asked my dad: "if everyone has two ears, two eyes, a nose, a mouth, how is that some people are pretty and others not?" He must have picked up on my insecurities that were driving my question as his reply was perfectly crafted. He told me that every person is beautiful in their own special way and no one else can be their kind of beautiful.

My father was like a lighthouse in my life, no matter how severe the storm, he stood tall and strong to give guidance and direction. He was well respected by many, truly a man of integrity.

Ex 20:12 "Honor your father and mother, so that you may live long in the land the Lord your God is giving you."

KAALVOET KINDERS

(Barefoot kids)

Life as a child, before earth became toxic through Covid-19

> *Growing up, playing in mud*
> *I saw no harm*
> *being on the farm*
> *to touch a baby pig*
> *then to pick a fig*
> *and eat the sweet treat*
>
> *Growing up, I saw no harm*
> *to hold a chicken*
> *before picking a peach*
> *and not to reach*
> *for water, washing hands*
> *after touching earth dirt*
> *that really didn't hurt*
>
> — *GROWING UP*

Mt 15:10 "Listen and understand. What goes into a man's mouth does not make him 'unclean' but what comes out of his mouth, that is what makes him 'unclean.'"

My piece of childhood paradise was a little farm, only five acres, near the Kalahari Desert. It was a small farming community that mainly grew corn and raised cattle, my parents kept chickens, piglets, sheep, and cows to milk. There was never a time we didn't have an exceptional garden. There were all kinds of fruit; figs, peaches, pomegranates, grapes, and the unforgettable strawberry fields, all sustained with water from the well and a wind pump.

The kids were up at dawn, picking ripe strawberries, then accompanied our father to milk cows and feed the chickens. The baby lambs were the cutest and got so excited to see us arrive with their bottles of milk, nudging each other out of the way to get first sips. My dad had black tea in the mornings and told the kids it was so that he can have his "shadow for the day", which is how he referred to his black tea or coffee before adding milk. Hearing that story, my own children wanted to have black tea with him so they could have shadows too.

Everyone in my family agreed the highlight of our family vacations were times spent at the community swimming pool by the lake, near to the town. My brother-in-law, Johan, and my sister, Lien, had a boat, to which they tied a big tube to the back and pulled the kids (and grown-ups) through the water for endless hours of fun. Evenings were BBQ time and my favorite part of the day, sitting around the fire and listening to its crackle and family conversations. These experiences added depth to my life that cannot be compared to anything else. Remembering the glow of flames, enhanced by brilliant stars and soft moonlight, bring memories of what was, but also a deep longing of what is no longer. But in the end, uplifting memories will stay, and burdensome longings fade away.

ACHILLE LAURO

Life can be so much fun
in the warmth of the sun
with the sky bright and blue
Your dreams may all come true
before this life is through

But thunder clouds will come too
before this life is through
It will not happen just to you
In ever life the rain must fall
to help us grow strong and tall

BEFORE THIS LIFE IS
THROUGH

La 3:33 "For He does not willingly bring affliction or grief to the children of men."

We usually spent Christmas time with the family, my parents-in-law had a big camper van and joined us on the farm. I had two fathers-in-law that came to spend this time together, and we all had a great time. The kids helped to pitch the tents under the big old thorn trees where they would sleep at night. They ran around barefoot all day and thus, occasionally stepped on thorns that fell from the trees, then ran to my mom in the kitchen for aid and sympathy. She would take the offending thorn from them and burn it in the coal stove and officiate the remedy with these words: "this thorn will never hurt you again" a ceremony that soothed aching bodies and minds.

My dad bred Chihuahuas and the kids spent endless hours in the dog pen playing with the puppies. But they were always eager, any time my dad called, to accompany him to town and visit my brother, Boeta, who was employed at the Theresa Hotel. Before the lounge got busy, Boeta invited the kids to the bar area, and allowed them to sit at the counter and served them cola. This special treat in adult territory made them feel real grown-up.

My husband and I sometimes used these visits at the farm as an opportunity for a short vacation ourselves, once we took a two-night cruise on the *Achille Lauro*. The day we were to board the ship, we first stood at the top of Table Mountain in Cape Town, looking over the ocean and seeing for miles, noticing there were no ships in sight, but didn't give it much thought. We were on time at the harbor to board but had to wait 5-hours before the ship finally arrived, delayed because of an onboard fire. The damp ship, wet from being extinguished still smelled of smoke. All the entertainment facilities were closed so we relaxed in the lounge at sunset and enjoyed watching dolphins play along the ship. At that time, we didn't know the history of the *Achille Lauro*. We went on the cruise in 1981, just after the fire and before Palestinian guerillas seized the ship, in both cases passengers died. I believe our cruise was with God's perfect timing to protect us from harm.

ACHILLE LAURO'S TUMULTUOUS PAST

The Miami Herald, Thursday 1 December 1994

[1947] Launched in Netherlands and named *Willem Ruys*.

[1953] Collides with her sister ship *Oranje* as they attempted to salute each other.

[1966] Neapolitan shipping magnate Achille Lauro bought both ships and renamed them. Both mysteriously then burnt and sink in a Sicilian port. They were later rebuilt.

[1970] *Achille Lauro* was outfitted for pleasure cruises.

[1971] The Liner rammed a fishing boat off the coast of Italy, killing a Neapolitan fisherman.

[1972] *Achille Lauro* caught fire again in Genoa, Italy.

[1975] *Achille Lauro* struck a Lebanese merchant vessel in Dardanelles off Turkey. 4 members of the merchant vessel were presumed drowned.

[1981] Fire broke out aboard the *Achille Lauro* off the Canary Islands. Panicked passengers jumped into the sea; two were drowned.

[1985] In October, Palestinian guerillas seized *Achille Lauro* in the Mediterranean and killed Leon Klinghoffer, a passenger, and dumped his body overboard in his wheelchair.

[1994] In June, Italy's neo-Fascist National Alliance charters the ship for a fund-raising cruise.

[1994] 30 November, *Achille Lauro* burned and sunk to its final resting place off Somalia.

EMPTY WALLS

If I can understand the reasons, I might find answers to my questions

> *If I can say "Because…"*
> *for every "Why?"*
> *and tell the truth*
> *instead of a lie*
> *I still can't give you*
> *every answer*
> *Because some questions*
> *Just don't have answers*
>
> — *QUESTIONS*

Ecc 7:10 "Do not say, "why were the old days better than these?" For it is not wise to ask such questions."

A cruel and barbaric method of execution became a favorite method of the terrorists, they called it 'necklacing' where a gasoline doused tire was placed around the victim's neck and set ablaze. This feared process was extremely intimidating, and the newspapers published numerous pictures of the victims, and all the other violence being perpetrated. As the danger worsened my husband began to think about immigration more seriously. We travelled to Botswana, Namibia, and Brazil, seeking a safe place to call home. Many who could immigrate at the time did.

Knowing what is right, and being able to do the right thing, does not mean it is easy to do. We believed there could be a better future for our children away from South African shores. However, the thought of leaving my life and all my family behind, was too harsh to contemplate. The uncertainties and complexities left me feeling vulnerable and weak. Helpless to stop my deepening worry, I found myself at the mercy of my dark thoughts and circumstances. How could I regain strength and have control over my thoughts? In my weakness, God's power grew.

2 Co 12:10 (b) "For when I am weak, then I am strong."

We lived eight years in our home by the stream but sadly, violence shattered our wonderful existence in that peaceful valley. When all was quiet you could hear the gentle sound of the stream, but after a heavy rain the gentle stream changed into a roaring river, in the same way my life also changed. The humidity was high the day we moved out of that house, the empty walls were wet and looked as if tears ran down the walls, just like the tears on my own cheeks.

1987 was coming to an end and we were on the verge of losing everything dear to us; our family, our homeland, and our life as we knew it. Feeling shaken and overwhelmed, I couldn't find the words to pray, and was barely able to hear God's soft voice or feel His gentle presence with me. But I know God never did or would abandon me.

ELIZABETH KIDSON

PRAYER

A language strange to human ears
is one thing that the devil fears
At times I cannot comprehend
all the words that God has sent

Though I do not understand
I know God is in command
and that will make the devil flee
so I can truly be at peace

A DIFFERENT
LANGUAGE

1 Co 14:13 "Anyone who speaks in a tongue should pray that he may interpret what he says. For if I pray in a tongue, my spirit prays but my mind is unfruitful."

1 Co 14:15 "So what shall I do? I will pray with my spirit but I will also pray with my mind."

I have met people so dear to me, I wanted to put my arms around them and hold them close, always, but as time passed, they eventually faded away into the past, leaving only their memories behind. I remember them all and won't forget the love and care they showed me. Each time I went through soul wrenching experiences, God sent someone to uphold me, pray with me, and encourage me. Thank God, my friend Dessie was with me during that awful time. He came to visit us every week and one day as we prayed together, he placed his hands on my head and asked God to fill me with the Holy Spirit. As he did, words came to mind that were unknown to me. I never forgot those words and often wondered what they meant.

Months later I recognized some of those words while reading

> "Kara" means to summon into a relationship
>   (adoption)
> "Yada" means to know intimately (oneness between
>   husband and wife)
> "Keya" means to praise with stretched out hands

>   EVERYMAN'S BIBLE COMMENTARY:
>   HOSEA AND AMOS

The Bible mentions two kinds of "Tongues" the one is a prayer language and the other one is to prophesy:

1 Co 14:2 "For anyone who speaks in a tongue does not speak to men but to God. Indeed no one understands him; he utters mysteries with his spirit."

1 Co 12:10 "...to another speaking in different kinds of tongues, and to still another the interpretation of tongues."

THE MIRACLE

We had a long journey ahead
and just a short prayer was said
Travelled at high speed in a car
our destiny was very far

There was danger at a certain place
but God is love, mercy, and grace
He had sent an angel to stay
and protect us along the way

After the dark of night
daybreak was a lovely sight
But suddenly a herd of cattle
and the sound of crushing metal

No-one was hurt, not a scratch
There is nothing on earth to match
God's love and His protection
in Him our plans reach perfection

AN ANGEL

Ex 23:20 "I am sending an angel ahead of you to guard you along the way."

It was early dawn and we were on our way to my dad's farm in our car, packed full of the few belongings we could take with us. The sun lit the white fog that settled on the black, freshly tarred road and just ahead two boys began to move a herd of cattle across the road. The black cattle on the black tar road on a white, misty morning made what happened next inevitable. When we were able to see what was ahead of us there was only seconds before impact.

My son was driving, I was sitting in the back, looking over his shoulder as I prayed, and I saw a path open up in the middle of the herd. Mick had little experience driving, but he stayed calm, held on tight to the steering wheel and didn't try to swerve to avoid a collision with the cows blocking our way. When the chaos ended, and our car came to a stop we were able to witness a miracle. The boys tending the cattle and all three of us in the car were safe with not even a scratch, but the car was badly damaged. If we had been injured at all, we wouldn't have been able to leave for America in four days.

We finally arrived at my parents' farm, it was the last point of preparation before departure and our last days in our homeland, it was the last of many beautiful things. We brought our beloved cat, Kieta, with us to live at the farm and it was a sad day when I picked her up for the last time.

BIBLE ROULETTE

My eyes rested sadly on the group
I'm feeling desperate as I stood
with my family so dear to me
and I wondered if I would ever see
them all again so dear to me

With heartbreaking emotions and fear
I prayed to God to dry up my tears
I kissed them and my eyes were dry
no, not one tear, I did not cry

One last gaze at the golden sand
before I must leave my homeland
without knowing where we'd go
I trust in God through every day
I know that He will show the way

— *NOT ONE TEAR*

Ps 86:6 "Hear my prayer, O Lord; listen to my cry for mercy. In the day of my trouble, I will call you, for You will answer me."

We were scheduled to leave for America on 23 December 1987. My mind knew we should go but my heart struggled to leave my two older children. Mick had one more year of mandatory military service to complete and the plans were for Mick and Nita to follow as soon as possible. This was a time of tremendous emotional turmoil, I cried out to God but found no comfort. It was already 21 December with only two more days until our departure.

As a young Christian I was often tempted to play Bible Roulette when going through difficult times. I opened my Bible and started to read and was amazed at what followed, and thereafter was greatly encouraged to take the journey ahead of me.

Jer 24:6,7 "My eyes will watch over them for their good, and I will bring them back to this land. I will build them up and not tear them down; I will plant them and not uproot them. I will give them a heart to know Me, that I am the Lord."

Jer 29:11 "For I know the plans I have for you, declares the Lord, plans to prosper you and not to harm you, plans to give you hope and a future."

According to these verses in Jeremiah, I believed it would be possible to return home to South Africa, but it never happened. There was never a time I could go back, always juggling commitments like loved-one's sick in hospital, anniversaries, weddings, or funerals. Years before, at my grandmother's funeral, I told my dad that I would never go to another funeral again, my words came true, but the funerals continued. I just couldn't go to be with my family during times of hardship, and they could not come to be with me.

LEAVING MY HOMELAND

Gone are all those familiar roads that led to familiar places

Those familiar roads
that led to familiar places
is where my soul found rest
and I was at peace

It was a heaven where I could go
and be part of something
much bigger than myself

When I lost those familiar roads
that led to familiar places
I lost my sense of belonging

Without those familiar roads
I didn't know where to go
and searched for my place in life
I was lost and so alone

FAMILIAR ROADS

Pr 13:12 "Hope deferred make the heat sick, but a longing fulfilled is a tree of life."

In my life I have moved around an awful lot. I lived by the desert, by the sea, in the mountains, by rivers and waterfalls, even stumbled into a lost little piece of paradise. I lived in big cities, small towns, and a farm. Being uprooted with every move, and once again leaving behind those familiar roads that lead to familiar places. Now we are in a foreign country, far away from my people and my homeland.

I have lived through so many experiences life has brought me, all having a profound impact on me. I feel that I have experienced a full range of the various facets of life. It is a privilege for me to be known well by people, those who listen from the heart to understand all I need them to know, and don't respond with their own agendas. People who understand the thoughts in my head even though no words were said between us.

I learned from my family to look at the bigger picture. During times that my mother was hospitalized, my grandmother and Aunt Miem took care of us. She usually took me to the dentist and helped to cover my schoolbooks. With the strong family ties that I was blessed with, being separated from them left deep and lasting wounds within me. That connectedness with my family was part of my daily life and now there was no more familiar food and family togetherness during celebrations and festive times. We yearned to be together but we couldn't, I had lost more than I ever thought I would by being separated from them.

Chapter Five

DIFFICULT ADJUSTMENTS

I am looking for God's presence in the unknown, the mysteries and paradoxes of my life.

DIFFICULT ADJUSTMENTS

It is an illusion to think one can hold on to anything, all we think we possess runs through our fingers like reflections in the water. Reflections are not real; it is only a shadow of what is real. Like reflections in the water, the illusion that I could hold on to what I had was shattered, and the familiar became the unfamiliar.

Often as a child I'd see
the reflection of trees
dancing on water in the night
as the moon shines bright

It's just a reflection

And just for a moment
I will see the movement
the reflection of birds in flight
flying through the night

But only for a moment

Reflections of my life
as a mother and a wife
brings melancholic thoughts to me
about people I love and cannot see

It is such a heartache

I pay the price of separation
with heartache and frustration
and melancholic thoughts
but for so much longer

Than just a moment

REFLECTIONS

Pr 15:13 "A happy heart makes the face cheerful, but heartache crushes the spirit."

Nothing good was coming to me at this point and had left me feeling discouraged. There was an uphill battle of difficult adjustments ahead of me, but despite the ups and downs, I never gave up, because I knew God would get me through it, a fact I had learned not to doubt.

FRANKFURT

With all my sorrows
and no tomorrows
Take me back home

I feel like dying

For all my crying
and all my sighing
Take me back home

— *SORROW*

Isa 40:31 "But those who put their hope in the Lord will renew their strength. They will soar on wings like eagles. They will run and not grow weary. They will walk not be faint."

My husband's childhood friend, Sam and his family, decided to immigrate with us, and the two families, ten in all, left South Africa on 23 December 1987. We spent the week between Christmas and New Year in Germany, Frankfurt is a beautiful city adorned with old buildings, but the days were cold and the skies were grey. I found the landscape both sad and poetic, a testament to our search of a safe home begun with hardly a ray of sunshine.

While in Germany we stepped out one afternoon for dinner but became lost on our way back to the hotel and found ourselves wandering through a 'red light area'. The twin boys, 12-years old at the time, could not believe their eyes and later that night, true to their nature, they snuck out to further investigate that area. They too became lost and as they were not fluent in English and couldn't speak any German, could not ask for help. When we noticed their absence, we ran through the streets looking for them, but to no avail. Fortunately, a couple of heaven-sent strangers who spoke English, assisted the twins and returned them safely to us.

We arrived in Miami from Frankfurt on New Year's Eve and almost immediately started looking for work and housing while the children spent their days playing on the beach. After a few weeks in Miami, we stored some of our luggage in a locker at the Amtrak train station. We took the train to Orlando to continue our search for a home, but we found no real opportunities there, so returned to Miami.

> *Give me not so little that I have to steal to survive*
> *And give me not so much that I forget why I'm alive*
> *(Pr 30:8)*

Pr 30:8 "Keep falsehood and lies far from me. Give me neither poverty nor riches but give me only my daily bread. Otherwise I may have too much and disown you. And say, "Who is the Lord?" Or I may become poor and steal and so dishonor the name of my God."

CAR JACKED

It was about 9 o'clock in the evening when we left our kids at the hotel room while we went to the Amtrak train station to collect our stored luggage. We're used to trains running twenty-four hours a day, seven days a week, and did not expect to find the station closed for the day. There was a man on the sidewalk, and we went over to talk to him when he confirmed the place was locked up for the night but offered to get the security guard to open the door for us. He disappeared around the corner and within seconds was back and explained that the security guard had already left.

Disappointed, we headed towards the car, but as I opened the door, I was pushed with such force I was thrown inside the car. A man grabbed my purse then ran to my husband and grabbed the car keys and his money. Sitting in the front seat of the car, dazed, and not fully grasping what was occurring, I came to my senses when the man jumped into the driver's seat and started the engine. I have no recollection of getting out of the car, I just remember standing next to my husband on the sidewalk as I watched the car speed away.

The police were there within minutes after we called them, helping us in any way they could. An officer was sent to the hotel room to keep the kids' company while we were delayed. After the police wrote down our statements, they took us back to the hotel and nicknamed us "the lucky couple." We were robbed and car jacked but were not hurt in any way. How ironic that we fled our homeland due to violence, only to experience violence in what was to be our refuge.

A friendly face
and a warm embrace
words truthful and kind
are so hard to find

TRUTHFULNESS

Ps 23:4 "Even though I walk through the valley of the shadow of death, I will fear no evil, for You are with me. Your rod and your staff they comfort me."

Towards the end of February, we moved into a town house in an area known as Cutler Ridge. There was a big open field in front of our townhouse where Sam and the kids had a lot of fun flying their kites. One day while the twins were flying a kite in the field, they crashed it into a neighbor's tree, and went to knock on the door to politely ask for permission to get their kite from the back yard. The lady who opened the door looked at my two sets of identical twins in utter disbelief, she thought it was a prank and looked up and down the street, expecting to see Candid Camera. Needless to say, we soon became good friends. Our neighbors held a big "Block Party" to welcome us to the neighborhood and introduced us to the people further down the road. We were grateful to find many friendly neighbors in our new community which made settling in easier.

TAKING RESPONSIBILITY

My dad used to say: "Help yourself and your friends will love you."

> *What I would like for me*
> *and for my family*
> *is not to go to neighbors*
> *at night or day for favors*
>
> *This is not pride my Lord*
> *I would just like to afford*
> *to pay my own way*
> *and a home where we can stay*
>
> *Friends that saw my need*
> *gave to me freely indeed*
> *Thank you for people who care*
> *when life is not so very fair*
>
> *I do not ask for luxury*
> *All I need is the ability*
> *to earn so I can give*
> *instead of to receive*
>
> *THE LORD*
> *PROVIDES*

Ps 37:25 "I was young and now I am old, yet I have never seen the righteous forsaken or their children begging bread."

. . .

Paul the Apostle taught by example that we as Christians should take responsibility to earn a living and not be a burden to others and lived by this edict by making tents to support himself while he was teaching the Word of God.

When we moved to America, we started off with almost nothing and were gifted furniture from neighbors and church, but slowly our situation started to improve. During this time my husband told me that between Jesus and myself we always had food on the table, at the time we didn't always have a table, but we always had food.

We were new to Miami and without a car. Behind our townhouse was a laundromat that belonged to Mr. Henry Johnson, an elderly Christian gentleman. The kids and I packed our laundry in suitcases and with a great team effort, took the shortcut over our wall to drop our washing. Going to Mr. Johnson was like going to a counselor, he took the time to listen to us all and offered good advice that helped me organize my thoughts and calm my emotions. After our laundry was cleaned, he usually helped us back over the wall to go home. When the kids started going to school, they always stopped by Mr. Johnson's Laundromat to say hello.

THE SLIDING SCALE

"Nothing under the sun is good or bad but thinking makes it so." —Shakespeare

> *We all have choices*
> *and all choices have consequences*
> *The choice to do nothing*
> *or the choice to do something*
>
> *What choices will I make*
> *as I ponder what the outcome may be*
> *Will choices I make today*
> *bring regret and sorrow tomorrow*
>
> > *CHOICES*

Dt 30:19 "See I have set before you life and death, blessings and curses. Now choose life that you and your children may live."

I had a peculiar dream one night, I saw 'innocence' depicted as snow, radiantly beautiful, dancing with 'malice' who looked greenish purple, like rotten meat, and held his tail between his fingers like a cigarette. Later, while pondering my dream, came the realization that the good and the bad in my life had become friends and danced together. This insight was a wake-up call for me. I justified my negative attitude by deflecting the blame and had viewed myself as an innocent, helpless bystander.

I don't know what the future may take away from me, there is nothing to do to stop it, but there is a lot not to do, by coping better. How can the occasional indulgence in self-pity turn into a destructive lifestyle? At what point does my faulty thinking become entrenched? It is such a gradual process, before that line between gratefulness and ungratefulness is crossed. I realized it happens when I fail to look past all the imperfections to enjoy what is truly beautiful.

As this journey with no end unfolds, my perception will change and eventually the pain will pass and the beauty will remain, but that cannot happen without my effort to make it so. I can always turn to God when right and wrong are so inextricably woven together, times when I can't define where the good ends and the bad begins. Now, when I am lost, I pray that God will pull my life apart and cleanse me of all my unrighteousness.

At times I can be so judgmental, with a tendency to compromise and resort to double standards. I didn't want to take responsibility for my role in my life situations, I preferred to avoid making difficult choices or confront my negative attitude. It was easier for me to ignore my indifference towards what would be helpful and what wasn't. I didn't want to look objectively to my life but choose to make excuses and place blame elsewhere. The positive made friends with the negative and danced together.

AVOIDANCE

My greatest regrets are not the wrong things I did but the right things I neglected to do

> *I think of all the time I waste*
> *I do nothing in a haste*
> *Always wait until tomorrow*
> *Often with regret and sorrow*
>
> *The bad habits God will show*
> *are often things I know*
> *but wouldn't like to admit*
> *Because then I will have to quit*
>
> *WASTING TIME*

Pr 24:33, 34 "A little sleep, a little slumber, a little folding of the hands to rest. So shall your poverty come like a prowler and your need like an armed man."

Soon after we were settled into our new home, my attention turned incessantly to my two eldest children that were left behind in South Africa. Plane tickets became my priority to bring us all together again, nothing mattered more to me. A lot of time was wasted by complaining and feeling sorry for myself that I couldn't bring them to me sooner, and I blamed myself for not succeeding sooner. This gnawed at my heart until I took responsibility and decided to do something about the situation.

It took a while before the twins could be registered in

school by which time it was too close to summer vacation for them to start. As they were not fluent in English, we decided it would be better for them to start in August with the beginning of the new school year. They were home for eight months and by then were ready for their new adventure, I was also eager to find work but being without a car my options were limited.

At the time, working at the Publix Supermarket was a good choice for me as it was within walking distance from my house. After my job application was handed in, it didn't take too long before my interview took place, and I was hired. My first day at Publix was a few weeks later, with an hourly rate of $4.00. After my savings account was opened, we started to save for the plane tickets. With a plan in place, I again began to feel optimistic about the future.

My beliefs determine my actions and as I change my beliefs, changes happen in my behavior. It was a long process and the changes come slowly, many times the right thing to do will be obvious to me, but I find it too difficult or uncomfortable to face at the time. My tendency to follow the way of the least resistance and sweep difficult situations under the rug has brought much sorrow to me, but I have come to learn that avoidance is never the right way, even though it's my favorite way.

LAUGHTER

Have you ever seen
a girl like Eileen
Her temper is frightful
but her laughter delightful

She can laugh away the storm
Makes the coldest heart feel warm

I hope that all her tomorrows
have little heartache and sorrows
and trust that she will find
Happiness and peace of mind

EILEEN

Ecc 3: "There is a time for everything and a season for every activity under heaven. A time to be born and a time to die. A time to plant and a time to uproot. A time to weep and a time to laugh. A time to mourn and a time to dance. A time to scatter stones and a time to gather. A time to embrace and a time to refrain. A time to search and a time to give up. A time to keep and a time to throw away. A time to tear and a time to mend. A time to be silent and a time to speak."

That was my time to make changes and adjust, not only to a job, but also to a new country with different values and life-style. It would be a long and hard journey but as I travelled along, I met people I will never forget. I felt they have special gifts they brought to me and it was exactly what I needed most during that time.

I was emotionally in an uncomfortable place with so much turmoil inside of me, and I struggled to leave my sorrow at home when I went to work. The memories dancing in my mind were filled with intense longing for what was but no more. During times when my days were bleak and void of pleasure, I found moments of laughter even more delightful to uplift my gloomy days.

A teenage girl came into my life at a time when I needed her joyful laughter to chase away the dark. She worked with me for a short time at Publix before moving on. I don't know where she went to, but I do know that she will always have her special place in my memory; the girl who brought me laughter when I needed it most. Thank you, Eileen.

A LOT TO LEARN

Two wrongs can never make one right

> *How can I get through*
> *to someone like you*
> *who will walk away*
> *and have nothing to say*
>
> *There is much frustration*
> *without good communication*
> *People always demand*
> *and I could not understand*

> *COMMUNICATION*

Heb 13:5,6 "Never will I leave you; never will I forsake you. So we say with confidence, The Lord is my helper, I will not be afraid. What can man do to me?"

In the beginning of my career at Publix, I was hoping to get a position as a florist which was my vocation in South Africa. Growing up we always had a beautiful flower garden, and we regularly went to pick wildflowers during springtime. These childhood experiences created within me a great love for flowers. I didn't enjoy my time in the Publix bakery and was a difficult adjustment for me. It was hard work with a lot to learn about many different products I hadn't even heard of before.

At the time my English was not fluent and it was difficult

to effectively respond to my co-workers and customers. They seemed not to care that I struggled, and so communicating was challenging. As time went by my position in the bakery improved when I began cake decorating, but it was still a challenge to communicate and adjust to the American culture. Enjoying the creativity, cake decorating turned out to be a wonderful career for me. Every morning I asked God to bless my work with satisfaction and giving my customers and co-workers a peaceful day.

My prayer for my work environment has always been: "Let there be peace in the bakery and let it begin with me."

As a Publix employee, I learned that it was better to lose an argument and save a relationship. This approach fits right into my inability to deal with disagreements in a constructive manner, I don't fight with my family, retaliate, or get into power struggles; two wrongs can never make one right. When a difference of opinion arises, the best thing for me to do is to step back and pray about the situation. Most of the time one of two thing will happen, given some time the issue will get resolved, and at other times the best approach will become obvious, but the challenge is then to take a stand and follow through with what should be done.

THE BAKERY

So many times, I wanted to leave
but, for some reason I just believed
there's no place like this anywhere else

So, I sat down and said to myself
"Why don't you give it one more day?
Tomorrow you might want to stay"

— *NO PLACE TO BE*

Php 4:7 "…and the peace of God which transcends all understanding will guard you hearts and your minds in Christ Jesus."

As a cake decorator, I experienced many wonderful moments with some great customers. Sometimes a customer would surprise me with a much-appreciated picture or two of their event. Weekends were our busiest times and I worked every Sunday, but usually finished my cake orders on time to take a couple of hours for church. After the service, I'd go back to work and finish my day. This dual shift on Sundays made for a long day, but thankfully it was possible to go to church and soon my friends expected to see me at church wearing my white cap and cake decorator uniform.

One morning while working on my orders, there was an order where the ticket indicated for a pentagram to be drawn as the decoration. I assumed this to be an error by the bakery clerk and prepared the cake with the "Star of David" as the design. When the customer saw the cake, she was furious and demanded to know how she could take a cake decorated with the "Star of David" to a Satanic Cult initiation ceremony. I couldn't believe my ears, and further that my co-workers didn't find this alarming.

It was rare for me to get a complaint from a customer in this instance I didn't mind receiving one. Clearly, there was a lot for me to still learn about the American culture. Being from a conservative Afrikaans upbringing, the pentagram incident shocked me and I refuse to have anything else to do with the cake, so my manager changed the symbol on the cake herself. Uncertain about what to do, but with a strong need to do something, I anointed the bakery with oil and asked one of my co-workers to pray with me.

Jas 4:14 (b) "…pray over him and anoint him with oil in the name of the Lord and the prayer offered in faith will make the sick person well."

THE WAITING

Ties that bind
each to his kind
Engraved in the mind
are the ties that bind

After many long years
through much anxiety and fear
I'm still waiting here

Behold through God's grace
I will see my loved one's face
On that day there will be no trace
of the sadness while I was waiting

— TIES THAT BIND

Zec 4:6 (b) "Not by might nor by power but by My Spirit says the Lord Almighty."

After what felt like an eternity, it was time for my eldest children to join us in Miami as there was enough money for the airfare, but then the unthinkable happened. The American Embassy refused to grant visas to Mick and Nita and just like that, they could not come. I woke up at night with the overwhelming experience that I had not woken from a nightmare and was living my days still stuck in an awful dream. This reality tormented me when I was awake and haunted me when I slept. Things took a turn for the worse when Mick was hospitalized with Rheumatic Fever after he completed his military service and spent weeks in hospital, without having the support of his parents. A nurse pushed him to the phone in a wheelchair when I called as he was too weak to walk, by that stage he weighed about a hundred pounds and it took months before he regained his strength.

The plan to get my children to Miami had to be postponed. Unfortunately, many overwhelming obstacles was to come to keep that from happening. As the pieces of my life fell irreversibly in place, one decision at a time, I was once again separated from Mick and Nita. My sister, Lien, has always been a second mother to my children and took care of them in my absence, she does not have children of her own and was happy to assist. After extensive medical treatment she eventually became pregnant but suffered a miscarriage and thereafter she gave up.

Persistence is perseverance and in time my children secured the necessary documents to come to America. With the funds already in waiting it seemed as if this crisis was all but over, but as chance would have it my daughter changed her mind about moving to Miami. She had met the man of her dreams and decided to settle down with him in South Africa. It was very difficult to accept that we could not be at my daughter's wedding and had to accept that I simply couldn't understand God's plan yet. My son, Mick, also married, but never had seconds thoughts about emigrating.

MYSTERIES AND PARADOXES

My mom used to say: "If you don't have what you like, then you better like what you have."

> *Discontent*
> *and his brother, Ungrateful*
> *and another*
> *whose name is Dissatisfied*
> *from them you have to hide*
> *in their company you will be*
> *miserable and defeated*
> *believe me*
>
> — *BE CONTENT*

Heb 13:5 "Let your conversations be without covetousness; and be content with such thing as you have."

Slowly my life started to improve, and I began to feel encouraged about the future once again. I love to read poetry and started to write my own when we came to America. A short sentence can paint a picture in your mind that speaks a thousand words. It's like a language sandwich where I pick the choicest words, wrap it up in a meaningful concept and end up with something to feed my soul. It clarifies my thinking and helps me focus on issues, most of my epiphanies came while reading or writing a poem.

To be happy is to be content, I cannot be content when my own belief system is betrayed.

· · ·

With more and more pieces being added to enrich the puzzle of my life, a bigger and clearer picture of God's purpose for me started to develop. The faulty decisions of my life caused much suffering but with courage I found hope, and with hope, in time, there was relief. God has good reason for not revealing the future to us and we don't need to know what the future holds. God is there and He safely holds me. I am looking for His presence in the unknown, in the mysteries and paradoxes of my life. In a place of stillness God will meet me and with trust I'll keep on focusing on His direction. My peace of mind comes through my relationship with God.

I can experience peace in times of sorrow, sickness, and trouble, I know this from personal experience. I doubt if it would have been possible for me to be here now if God did not guard my mind and hold me safely in the palm of His hand, as death and destruction awaited me just around the corner.

1 Ti 6:6 "But godliness with contentment is great gain. For we brought nothing into the world and we can take nothing out of it."

Chapter Six

DEATH AND DESTRUCTION

...and suddenly my child is gone, and the chair empty.

A LONELY PATH

"Anyone can master grief but he who has it." —Shakespeare

The path is lonely and narrow
My only companion is the sparrow
God knows, He can tell
of everyone that ever fell
to the ground where grass grows

Life is as transient as grass
and the shadows it cast
before the wind blows it away
You may know love today
but it could be gone tomorrow
Leaving you with memories and sorrow

You may seek but you will not find
the life that passed away
All that is left behind
are the memories that weigh
so heavy on your mind

SHIFTING SHADOWS

Ps 103:15 "As for a man, his days are like grass, he flourishes like a flower of the field; the wind blows over it and it is gone, and its place remembers it no more."

Our second year in Miami did not go well. Towards the end of May my sister called from South Africa to tell me that my favorite cousin, Henning, had died in a car accident. As a teenager he lived with us for a while, we were best friends and always went out with the same group of friends. The two of us remained close until we immigrated to America, his unexpected death was devastating news to me.

A few months later, just before Christmas, my father-in-law died. He was on his way to visit my parents on the farm, when he lost control of his car, it overturned, and he died instantly. He lived with us during the years my kids grew up and was very much part of our lives. These accumulated losses were extremely hard to cope with.

SUICIDE

> *Birds with broken wings*
> *live with the pain it brings*
> *They want to fly*
> *high up in the sky*
> *endlessly free....*
> *but they cannot be*
> *with broken wings*

— *BROKEN*
WINGS

Ecc 1:15 "What is twisted cannot be straightened; what is lacking cannot be counted. (Everything is meaningless)"

My brother, Boeta, was 6-years old and wouldn't walk due to a painful problem with his hips. He spent one year in an orthopedic hospital and so missed his first year of school. It was not possible for us to visit him regularly, and the abandonment and loneliness he experienced robbed him of a normal childhood and the ability to adjust to life outside the hospital walls. He was released from hospital at the time my sister passed away and was reunited with his family at a time when everyone was in deep mourning, making a joyful return impossible. This was a time he needed our full attention to help him adjust, but we couldn't support him when we were battling to support ourselves.

This additional separation and isolation created an ongoing challenge for him to fit into the school routine as he grew older and as a teenager he struggled with depression. Through the years we did our best to encourage him during those episodes, at times we invited him to visit with us and the changes of scenery seemed to help, but he never wanted to stay for long. His nephews and nieces adored him, and he loved them just as much.

Eventually he took his own life, three years after we emigrated. I felt if we had been there, close to him, we could have intervened just as we did so many times before. The guilt and regret were almost unbearable, and I had to learn to block any thought that started with "what if" or "If only." Thought stopping was a difficult discipline to master but I had to persist for my own sanity.

The suicide note addressed to my parents asked this question:

My Mom and my dad,
Did you ever think what will happen to me once you are gone?
I am so sorry.

Years later, November 1999, my aunt Maggie committed suicide as well. This was easier for me to accept since she was a nurse with Parkinson's disease. She knew what awaited her and when things progressed too far for her, she shot herself when she was home alone. I could understand her decision.

THE ELEPHANT

Life was suddenly consumed by the torment and comfort that occurs by living in memories. My earliest memory of my brother, Boeta, is when he was 18-months old. The circus came to town, bringing with it great excitement that we could barely contain while standing in line, waiting to be seated.

Suddenly a circus elephant took my brother out of my dad's arms, held him up in the air, then placed him back in my dad's arms. In shock we stood there and watched but cannot even tell you how my parents responded. My mind couldn't register anything else. My parents were probably horrified one moment and intensely relieved the next. They never discussed the event in front of me, probably one of those happenings they wanted to forget.

My brother was one of those unfortunate tortured souls. I experienced some of that emotional anguish when I was in my twenties but found God's truth before life's lies destroyed me. It was a very difficult journey for me but I made it through and believed that my brother would as well. I tried to go back to that state of despair I experienced so long ago, in a desperate search of understanding to ease my grief but couldn't stay there long. Working through my own pain gave me a greater clarity of his struggles. Even though I may not fully understand how he could have taken his own life, I had great compassion for his suffering.

Boeta told me more than once that he had to stop being bad before he could go to God. He could not understand that he needed God first so that God could change his life and make it good. There was a barrier between himself and the rest of the world that couldn't be broken, that emotional detachment made it impossible for me to get through to him.

I love cats
but I hate it
when cats catch birds
because I love birds too
God loves the sinner but hates the sin

CATS AND BIRDS

Jn 8:32 + 36" ...then you will know the truth, and the truth will set you free. (36) If the Son sets you free, you will be free indeed."

I had a lot of guilt to deal with, Boeta's death crushed my heart but there was not much time to grieve for him. Two weeks later, 30 April, my 15-year-old son, Laurence, was murdered.

EMPTINESS

Then suddenly my son is gone, and the chair empty

My children were always home before dark and when the day started to close and Laurence had not returned, his siblings went to look for him. Their friend from church drove them to the house of a friend to look for Laurence. When they arrived there, they found that the area had been sealed off with yellow tape. The police told them someone was killed and instructed them to go home after exchanging contact information.

By the time they were home the event was all over the afternoon news: *"Unidentified 15-year-old boy shot and killed"*. Helpless and anxious my children waited at home hoping Laurence would return soon. My husband and I came home late from a school meeting and when we walked through the door the kids told us that Laurence went jogging and never came home. I stayed home with the kids while my husband went to the police station.

It was 30 April 1991. Two weeks earlier Laurence was nominated as Student of the Year. He won awards for every section he was entered in. He had told his teacher, Mr. Peoples: "My mom is so sad because her brother died. All these trophies I had won will make her so happy." Laurence and I worked together at the same Publix so he could earn extra money. Many times, he would bring me coffee with a hug and a kiss, my manager would jokingly tell him we don't allow kissing on the job.

During that time Laurence always wanted to sit between my husband and myself, it didn't matter where we were, at home or out, he would fight for that place between us. And then suddenly, he was gone, and the chair empty.

We all sit around the table
but nobody is able
to mention the chair
the empty chair
and pretend it's not there

Tonight nobody fights
to sit there
in the empty chair
the empty chair
between my husband and I
and I hung my head and cry

—— THE EMPTY
CHAIR

Ps 6:6-7 "I am worn out from sobbing. All night I flood my bed weeping, drenching it with my tears. My vision is blurred with grief."

I DON'T KNOW

Into the mouth of death
my son walked
and was swallowed up

With his last breath
he could not talk

In an instant, he died
and could not say goodbye
before he was swallowed up.

— *THE MOUTH OF*
DEATH

Jas 1:13–15 "Nor does (God) tempt anyone; but each one is tempted when, by his own evil desire he is dragged away and enticed. Then after desire has conceived it gives birth to sin, and sin, when it is full-grown, gives birth to death."

Time became a blur of pain, endless hours lying in bed sobbing and wishing reality away. During the next few weeks, the police worked diligently to uncover the events that ultimately took our son, which became a lifeline of information and justice in a time where nothing made sense anymore. From what we managed to uncover, Laurence had gone to check on his friend, Jeff, who had missed school for a few days. It turned out that Jeff's home had been burglarized several times during the past few weeks, and his father decided to keep his son home to guard the house, giving him a weapon and ammunition for this task.

That night Jeff admitted to the police that he had placed a bullet into the gun and shot Laurence in the head at close range. In an attempt to hide his actions, he dragged my son's body to the front door, changed clothes and took his dog for a walk. After he had returned from his walk, he called his father then dialed 911 to report an attempted robbery.

As advised by his father, Jeff told the police he believed my son was a burglar and had shot him by accident. Jeff kept to his story while he was with his father, but confessed a different story once separated from him and questioned about inconsistencies in his story. When the officer asked him what motive he could have had to shoot Laurence, Jeff said he just didn't know.

Laurence died instantly, he was sitting on the couch and reading a magazine and did not even hear the shot. After all the court proceedings were finished, Jeff was sentenced 500 hours of community service for killing my son, and his father was sentenced 500 hours community service for leaving weapons and ammunition in the care of his 14-year-old son. Jeff was not allowed back to Centennial Middle School; he was transferred to another school in a different town where nobody knew him. My husband tried to keep this murder on Jeff's record, but it was not allowed, the case was closed and filed away. I thank God that Laurence died without fear, without pain, and without knowing his death was imminent. There were no fights or harsh words between Lawrence and myself to regret, allowing me to grieve my son without the sting of unresolved issues.

MY HIDING PLACE

He walks on streets of gold
while I walk on streets of dust
and in my mind his memory I hold
as I walk, carried by my trust
that through God's grace
we will meet again
and walk-through God's place
but until I can go home
I'll walk on streets of dust
all alone.

STREETS OF GOLD

Rev 21:21 "The twelve gates were twelve pearls, each gate made of a single pearl. The great street of the city was of pure gold, like transparent glass."

Lawrence's memorial service was on Friday 3 May, at the Cutler Ridge United Methodist Church. The church was full to the rafters, leaving only standing room for all those who came to mourn him. Our community gathered in shock and pain to support us, and we were amazed at the outpour of sympathy. Our home quickly filled with gifts of flowers, cards, donations, and food. As an immigrant family who moved here only a few short years ago, people from the Church, Centennial Middle School, and Publix all came to help us through the unthinkable. Devastated in grief, we did not feel alone.

Laurence's teachers Mr. Peoples and Ms. Propeck ceremoniously laid a plaque and planted a tree in front of the school in memory of Laurence. Special arrangements were made at a very late stage to add an extra page in the yearbook. His friend wrote a poem and we gave the school a picture of Laurence to use in the yearbook, one of my favorite pictures of him; he sits in the little white Yugo, his car that he was still making payments on. He couldn't wait to get his driver's license, and sadly he didn't, he died 10 weeks before his sixteenth birthday.

The following months were difficult, life soon returned to normal for everybody else but for us. It was unbearable to be home alone and we had no family or close friends to spend time with. I found myself wandering around aimlessly at the mall on my days off from work, I didn't want to stop moving because if I did, the grief overwhelmed me. Sometimes I'd go to the bakery to spend time with my co-workers during their lunch breaks. The bakery became my hiding place, an escape from my reality. My work and the bakery remained normal while the rest of my life was an unfamiliar nightmare. The bakery provided me with the desperately needed stability during this time.

Through the help of friends, we found our way to bereavement support groups called 'Parents of Murdered Children' and 'Compassionate Friends.' Together, the bereaved found support as we gathered to share understanding and guidance.

HIS LAST WISH

Mothers do not love one child
more than the others
But sometimes one child
can support his mother
more than his sister or brother
can support their mother

Did he perhaps know
that it was almost time to go?

— CHILDREN

1 Co 13:7 "(Love) always protects, always trusts, always hopes, always perseveres. Love never fails."

Laurence took it upon himself to help me buy his sister, Nita, and her husband, Cecil, plane tickets to America. He saved money by working at Publix as a bag boy and cleaning up at the local hair salon for extra money. By the time Nita and Cecil could visit, Laurence had already saved up $1000 to help buy the plane tickets. The day we went to the bank, to withdraw the money from his savings account, he told me it was his contribution to the family and did not want the money returned.

We could never pay him back and his sister could never thank him as only 2-weeks later he died. As it happened his memorial cost $1000, the irony of this hurt me deeply. I felt he had paid for his own funeral; we weren't able to offer the last gift of his funeral to him.

Nita and Cecil visited a few short weeks after his death in May 1991. Their visit made Mother's Day tolerable but the tragedies kept on coming. During their visit my sister, Lien, called from South Africa to tell us that my aunt Miem had died from jaundice. She had provided me with much stability during my childhood and always took care of us when my mom was unable to.

6-months after she passed, my uncle Dawie suffered a fatal heart attack. We shared a special bond between us, he patiently answered all my childhood questions and was always willing to lend his ear. When we once visited him on the Botswana border, I found it fascinating to see him 'read' all the animal tracks in his surroundings and like always, answer all my questions about the ways of the desert. He still called me "Books" by my childhood nickname he gave me.

It was a time of profound sadness and I was drowning in loss upon loss.

Isa 57:1 (b) "Devout men are taken away, and no-one understands that the righteous are taken away to be spared from evil."

GOD, WHY?

I tried to understand but I couldn't and kept asking God, "why?" I begged him to help me, to explain how this could have happened. I was deeply confused and all the pain and loss had shaken my faith to the core. Throughout the years as my children grew, God had intervened miraculously so many times to keep them safe. I kept on thinking of all the times death approached my children but no serious harm had come to them, it was a miracle that they were never seriously injured.

One day the four twins were playing by the backyard slope which led down to the river. They were rolling big rocks downhill and took turns diving out of the path of the tumbling rocks. Angie waited too long before diving away and was hit by one of them. It hit her so hard on her head that she rolled unconscious right down to the river, but the bushes along the riverside stopped her from rolling into the river. Laurence, Duncan, and Jeanette frantically ran to get Mick, they thought they had killed their sister as all they could see were her legs sticking out from the bush. Mick ran to rescue Angie, he climbed down the steep hill, picked her up and climbed his way back up the slope. She became semi-conscious halfway up and started to blindly fight Mick, leaving him struggling to make it back up the slope. Angie had a fractured skull, a bruised brain, lots of stitches, and two huge black eyes, yet after a while in hospital, made a full recovery.

A few years after this incident my four twins were walking home from school, Laurence, Duncan, and Jeanette crossed the road safely but Angie hesitated. She saw a gap and took it but was hit by a car. The impact threw her up in the air, flying over the roof of the car and landed behind the car holding tightly to her book bag, which made a safe cushion to land on and protected her from serious injuries while skidding along the road. As soon as she came to a standstill she got up and started to look for her shoe which had flown off from the impact, she had a lot of road rash from the accident but still attempted to continue walking home. A shocked bystander stopped her and called an ambulance to take her to the hospital. After proper examination, the doctors couldn't find anything wrong with her other than the road rash and sent her home with a few Band-Aids.

During those days I never knew what to expect, returning home from a doctor's appointment one afternoon I was approached by my neighbor. She told me that they found my son Laurence, bleeding profusely from his upper arm. While visiting a friend, he was bitten by their Rottweiler, 11-years old at the time, he would have had to walk quite a distance to get home. He needed immediate medical attention, so our neighbor Malcolm took him to the doctor. I was intensely grateful for their help and went right back to the doctor's office. Laurence lost a lot of blood and needed stitches, but he recovered fully with barely a scar to show.

So many of these incidents kept bubbling in my mind. With all the hospital trips, through all the illnesses and accidents, no permanent damage was experienced by my children. Then Laurence died. God had intervened so many times before, why not this time? I tried hard to understand but I couldn't find peace. Then slowly I began to realize that life on earth is a journey and for some, a shorter one than for others. Laurence is home already; I am not home yet.

Ps 139:16 (b) "All the days ordained for me were written in Your book before one of them came to be."

TRUTH

One cannot ask insightful questions when there's no under-
standing of what the matter is all about

> *I asked God for understanding*
> *He brought me to your door*
> *and as I trusted you more and more*
> *you gently encouraged me to explore*
>
> *But I was not prepared*
> *for questions that evade me*
> *and answers I couldn't see*
> *I sat there in the chair*
> *my hands in my hair*
> *and struggle to get insight*
> *but it's just not there*
> *try as I might*
> *I can't get it right*
>
> *I ask for understanding every time I pray*
> *But God…*
> *thank you for the teacher anyway*
>
> — *UNDERSTANDING*

Questions about the future lie in past experiences, but I often
fail to grasp the revelations. My life is based on truth with an
honest search for answers, but there are times when reality
becomes too much. Memories in the fragments of my mind
are peaceful escapes with gentle colors and slow movements.

It's not real though, only reflections of what once was real. But like illusions, even though it's not truth, it softens reality.

At times I want to re-write reality just a little bit. Illusions are just beautiful lies at times when truth is unbearable and facts too harsh to tolerate. Then denial comes in like a welcome friend to soften the blow and gives an invitation to disappear into the world of illusions. It might be a good place to rest for a while, but not to stay. Eventually, reality needs to be faced before life can continue.

Life and death are a paradox, the one contains the other. Paradoxes teach balance as both are true but opposite expressions. One cannot exist without the other one. It is necessary for me to have a balanced view on life and to look at both sides, the positive and the negative, and how one fits into the other and together become complete.

Ps 42:1 "As a deer pants for streams so my soul thirst for you, O God. My soul thirst for God, for the living God."

FEELING OF WELL-BEING

I will let good thoughts settle into my mind and become part of my mental process

> *There are times*
> *I have these feelings of well-being*
> *as good thoughts flood my mind*
> *And like colorful starbursts*
> *brighten up my dark emotions*
>
> *— STARBURSTS*

Php 4:8 "Whatever is true, whatever is noble, whatever is right, whatever is pure, whatever is lovely, whatever is admirable—if anything is excellent or praiseworthy—think about such things."

4:9 (b)" ...and the God of peace will be with you."

The best place to be in times of sorrow has always been at church, there is just something healing about being in the company of fellow Christians, rather than being home alone, and so it was one evening, a few months after my son was killed. Feeling mentally exhausted with little strength left to continue, I needed to be at Church more than anywhere else. I had reached my end and couldn't go on any further, carrying my cross of loss.

At Church we sang the song *It is well with my Soul* when a man I have never seen at church before entered the back door. He was dressed in blue jeans and a black tee shirt and around his neck he wore a silver cross. This stranger approached me and we had a pleasant, but brief, conversation. He didn't say much, just looked into my eyes, took the cross off his neck, and placed it around mine. Then he turned around, walked away, and I never saw him again.

But something amazing happened as he walked away; it was as if he took with him my heavy cross of anguish that had all but crushed me and replaced it with one I could manage. Through the years, every time I hold this silver cross in my hands, or wear it around my neck, I am reminded of this remarkable encounter with a man who didn't say much but made such a difference.

I often wonder about this stranger, was it perhaps someone who knew Laurence? Or maybe he was just someone who was sent by God.

Mt 10:38 "Anyone who does not take his cross and follow Me is not worthy of Me."

HURRICANE ANDREW

Hurricane Andrew struck in August of 1992, and the destruction it caused was beyond belief. If you could have looked in my heart after Laurence was killed, you would have found a similar state of desolation, if not worse.

> *My name should be…melancholy…*
> *Content to be sad*
> *turning every good thought to bad*
> *Melancholy appears when peacefulness nears*
> *and brings dark and gloom*
> *It always comes too soon and lingers far too long*
> *until all joy is gone, it is my folly*
> *My name should be…melancholy*

> — *MELANCHOLY*

14-months after Laurence passed away, my son Mick and his wife, were finally able to move to America. They arrived at Miami Airport on 23 June 1992 and the whole family were there to welcome them. To celebrate, we all went to Orlando for vacation in late August 1992. We did not get to do many activities as the weather was heavy with rain day after day. In shock we watched the news on TV as weather anchors reported from Black Point Marina about a dangerous hurricane aiming directly at our home. The morning of 24 August Hurricane Andrew made landfall as a category 5. The eye of the storm hit Miami at 4:52 am as we watched the news anxiously for updates. With 168 mph winds, the devastation was shocking and stretched for miles and miles.

As soon as the roads allowed residents of the area to return, we came home to see what the impact would be. It was an eerie drive home as we looked at the damage and couldn't recognize landmarks in our own neighborhood. We felt like foreigners in a war-torn, getting lost on roads that had completely changed and felt unfamiliar. Everything had been blown away, even Mr. Johnson's Laundromat.

We found our neighborhood almost completely abandoned, with only four families left of which two of the men were Vietnam Vets. They helped us survive the aftermath of the storm with their survival skills; our neighbor Paul took it upon himself to guard our property with a shotgun to keep looters at a distance. Our home was in bad shape with most of our belongings damaged or destroyed. With part of the roof gone, the ceilings collapsed, and the windows shattered. Most of the doors inside the house were ripped out of their frames. Standing in the midst of all the destruction, I could only imagine the terror we would have endured if we had remained at home during the hurricane.

Nu 6:24-26 "The Lord bless you and keep you. The Lord makes His face shine upon you and be gracious to you. The Lord turns His face toward you and give you peace."

A TREE PLANTED

Out of all the devastation God sent a lot of help, it was a time when people came together and helped each other. In the evenings we cooked outside on a grill, enjoying the good company. Without city lights to blur the sky, for the first time since we left South Africa, we could see the stars again. It took me back to the time on my father's farm where we sat outside next to the fire eating and sharing stories. Unfortunately, our friendship with Sam and his family, who had emigrated when we did, faded away during all the chaos after the hurricane. For the longest time they were the only people we knew and who spoke our language, but after the hurricane they moved to the Keyes. The end of one friendship was the beginning of another, I met Jean at church, she was one of the lucky few who had electricity and invited me to her home to take hot showers and do laundry. In her, I am blessed with a special and enduring friendship.

For months we lived without windows, doors, or electricity, fortunately, we always had running water. When the contractors began work on our home we had nowhere to go and so lived in the downstairs section while they worked upstairs and moved upstairs while they worked downstairs. Thanks to our pastor, Tom Woodard, we were 'adopted' by Sanibel Community Church, who helped us replace our furniture and household appliances. After we were connected to electricity again, we all retreated into the indoor comforts that come with powered appliances. The electric frying pan and slow cooker made cooking possible during the times we had to cook in the bathroom during the renovation.

Our neighborhood slowly but surely began to rebuild, but there were still houses that remained devastated and unrepaired, they looked similar to my grieving process. As our surroundings improved, my life also started to slowly improve.

Occasionally we would pass by a storm-destroyed house, in the same way I would hear or see something that brought a flood of pain washing through my body, leaving me as undone as all those houses. Hurricane George struck seven years after Laurence was killed, it did not cause too much damage, but it did uproot the tree that was planted in my son's memory. Driving by and seeing the uprooted tree did not upset me nearly as much as the yellow tape that surrounded it. It resembled the yellow tape that marked the house where my son was killed. This reminder hit me with a sudden and intense pain, sobbing uncontrollably, I had to pull off the road where it took a while for me to feel well enough to carry on driving. My son's life was cut short in his prime and so was the tree planted in his memory.

So many tears that must be cried
are all still pent up inside
Pleasant feelings anchored down
by heartache and fear
into the tears they sank
drowned…and died…

— *TEARS*

2 Co 5:17 "If anyone is in Christ, he is a new creation; the old has gone, the new has come."

Chapter Seven

IMMIGRATION

The end of one journey is the beginning of another.

THIS IS THE WAY

Immigration laws have changed a lot during the years, we read stories regularly in the daily papers about people caught up in an unforgiving immigration system. These stories caused tremendous stress and made it clear that we could not go back to South Africa to visit our family. As a result, it was six years from the time we left before I saw my parents again. It was 1994, everyone came to see the first child in our family born in America. We had a wonderful time reconnecting and enjoying each other's physical presence, but sadly, we never saw my parents or parents-in-law again. My father-in-law died from kidney failure shortly after their visit and my mother-in-law, paralyzed after a series of strokes, died in February 1999.

This is the way to go
though it may be painful and slow
Even when doubt make you frown
A godly journey insures a crown

-- THE WAY

Mt 4:7 "Do not put the Lord your God to the test."

My son, Mick, applied for permanent residence and was waiting for his interview with the INS. In the past, the applicant could pay a fine of a thousand dollars and be allowed to stay in America until the immigration papers were done. However, since April 1997, applicants were given 6-months to get their papers processed. If their papers were not processed within that time (due to a back log at the immigration offices) the applicant had to return to his country of origin and wait there for an interview. The INS was not able to process Mick's application in time and he had to return to South Africa with his wife and their American born son.

Appeals were filed and we continued to pray. The plane tickets were booked for 24 September which was a required condition to file the appeal. Once again being tempted to play Bible Roulette, I prayed and opened my Bible, and started to read Hag 2:18, 19 (b) *From this day on, this twenty-fourth day of the ninth month...until now, the vine and the fig-tree, the pomegranate and the olive tree have not borne fruit. "From this day on I will bless you."*

24 September, what are the odds? I believed God promised me a miracle. Even at the airport as we watched my son boarding the plane, I believed we would receive the call from the attorney telling us that he didn't have to go, but the call never came. His application to stay in America was approved two months after the deadline. It was a common experience for immigrants who work their way legally through the immigration process. Those who didn't leave by the deadline and received their approval late, benefit from it by keeping their employment and incurring no relocation costs. Those who left on time received no benefits, were not allowed to come back until their interviews, and incurred a heavy financial burden.

THE VISIT

I was deeply disappointed when my son had to return to South Africa. We called my sister, Lien, and told her Mick and his family were on their way and asked her and my brother-in-law to pick them up at the airport. Lien and Johan helped them as best they could, in hindsight, much good came from Mick's return to South Africa as they had opportunity to visit with various family members.

Sadly, this was my father's last few months with his family before he passed away. Many times, during my life, instead of gaining encouragement from a Bible verse, my selfishness and fear alters the message to one that my heart desires. By placing my own interpretation to these verses, I created my own expectations. Now, knowing that God will always act in my best interest, I have learned not to look for promises in writing.

Thank God, during this time my daughter Nita and her family arrived from South Africa to visit us. It was with great excitement that we met my two grandsons for the first time. Vincent was 3-years old and Grenwill was 2-years old. We had much fun doing everything we possibly could and took a fair number of pictures, most of which were taken at Disney World, which was definitely the highlight of their visit.

As Halloween is not celebrated in South Africa, my grandsons didn't know much about the holiday and were scheduled to return home just before Halloween. To let them experience the fun, we dressed them up in their Halloween costumes and took them to the mall to 'trick or treat' where we explained to the friendly people at the mall that they were leaving in a few days and were having their very own mini-Halloween, to which everybody played along. With growing excitement Vincent and Grenwill watched as their little pumpkins filled up with sweets and treats. Sadly, time flew by too quickly and soon the day came when it was time to take them back to the airport and for us to return to a quiet, empty house.

> *It is quiet all around*
> *and in my loneliness*
> *I need*
> *the pleasant sound*
> *of little feet*
> *that are so far away*
> *To come*
> *and tiptoe through my day*
>
> — *LITTLE FEET*

Isa 55:9 "As the heavens are higher than the earth, so are My ways higher than your ways, and My thoughts than your thoughts."

FORTY-HOUR FAST

My son waited 8-months for an interview with the American Embassy and was finally scheduled for Monday, 18 May 1998. The week before their interview I asked my Christian friends to pray with me, we asked God for the right immigration officer to conduct the interview and that Mick would answer correctly and well. I fasted 40 hours, from Saturday afternoon until Monday morning to show my commitment to my prayers. At 3:00am (9:00am South African time) while kneeling in my closet, praying, Proverbs 31:25 came to mind, peace came over me, I went to bed and slept till morning.

Pr 31:25 "She is clothed with strength and dignity. She can laugh at the days to come."

The phone rang earlier Monday morning than we expected when a very excited Mick told me the interview was supposed to be from 8.30 am till 12:00pm (South African time) but the officer who was scheduled for the interview was not available, rather the head of the department had taken his place. My daughter-in-law was pregnant and they did not have any time to spare, it was crucial that they finalized their immigration meeting, got the paperwork completed, and returned to America. The officer asked my son why he wanted to go to Miami, to which he replied that he had a great job offer there. The officer then asked if my son liked Miami to which my son cheered: "Go Dolphins!" Showing support and appreciation for the Miami Dolphins Football team was clearly a great answer, my son had a positive and friendly interview.

God looked down
And placed on my head
A victory crown

— *VICTORY*

Ps 145:18 "The Lord is near to all who call upon Him."

Mick and his family arrived back in Miami on 26 May 1998, the same day as my 25th Wedding Anniversary. While in South Africa they attended my parents 50th Wedding Anniversary and brought with them the precious gift of family photos and videos of the anniversary ceremony. Two weeks after their return we received a call from my daughter, Nita, in South Africa. It was a Thursday afternoon, 11 June, she told me that my dad was hospitalized two days previously with pneumonia and had taken a turn for the worst.

That evening at 8:30pm, she called again to tell me my dad had just passed away. My sister Lien, and her husband Johan were with him until the end. Lien told me later how my father had struggled to breath the last two days but still prayed for his family. I love my dad so much; it is still hard to believe that he is gone and we couldn't see him one last time. My sister promised to bring my mom with them to spend some time with us in America, but my mother didn't stay long enough for that visit. A year later, on 28 July my mother suddenly died from a heart attack, or possibly from a broken heart. She died on what would have been the birthday of my brother who had committed suicide.

OUR DAY IN COURT

I know about today
but cannot truly say
That I will be here
next week, next year

I have not been told
what the future may hold
Although I sometimes care
My God makes me aware
The path is always there

I have seen too much of God not to trust Him

— I KNOW

Isa 58:9 "Then you will call, and the Lord will answer, you will cry for help, and He will say: "Here am I""

Our process with the INS continued to build with concern and stress, for a while I would wake up at night from anxiety. One night as I was lying in bed praying, asking God to open a door for us to get out of this stressful situation, my bedroom door opened. Even if the wind had pushed the door open, God could use wind as His messenger. God listens to my prayers and nothing can stop His plans. Duncan pursued his path to citizenship while our applications were making their way through the system faster than we could find a way to avoid deportation, however, we were running out of time.

In a desperate effort our attorney filed the papers for Duncan to sponsor us before he was able to establish citizenship. The hope was that our application process for sponsorship, would give us the time we needed for Duncan to become a citizen so that he could sponsor us. Unfortunately, time was working against us. We were ordered to court to plead our case which had a high possibility of failure as Duncan was not yet a citizen. The result would be deportation for us. As our attorney explained this to us, I mentioned to him that my Christian friends were praying for us, he replied, "From your lips to God's ears" but he cautioned that our case did not look good.

Our court date came too fast, with my son's application for citizenship still being processed, we arrived with our lawyer and prayers. Miraculously important documents were missing from our court records and the judge had to reschedule our hearing for a later date when all the necessary papers were in order. As we were leaving the courtroom I said to our attorney "From my lips to God's ear", he gave me a big smile. With the extra time granted to us, Duncan was able to complete his own citizenship.

PUBLIX SHOOTING

If I can go back
Into times of long before
My heart would be poor of wishes
And truly wish no more

— *WISHES*

Ps 42:5 "Why are you downcast, oh my soul? Why so disturbed within me? Put your hope. In God for I will yet praise Him."

I often wondered if perhaps Laurence would be alive today if we had stayed in South Africa. But how much control do we really have over life and death? We do not regret our decision to come to Miami, even though we lost Laurence here. In South Africa, it didn't seem safe anywhere and my son could have been killed there just as he was in America.

From time to time, we were harshly reminded of the reason we fled our homeland. My uncle, Visser, was a building contractor and one Friday afternoon he was attacked by two men as he was getting ready to pay his workers. They stabbed him with knives, took his money and guns, and left him for dead after they locked him in the gun safe. Even though the contract workers came to his rescue and rushed him to hospital, he didn't survive. A few years after this attack, my cousin, Bennie, who lived on a farm, was ambushed, robbed and murdered on the dirt road close to the farmhouse. Probably by some of the farm workers who knew him.

It is both tragically coincidental and ironic to flee from

violence to seek safety, only to find more violence. The holiday season arrived that year lacking in excitement, with the recent passing of my father, it was difficult to muster joy. It was the day before Christmas and I couldn't call home to speak to him. The bakery was bustling with cake orders, but I was oblivious to the holiday festivities, mechanically going through the motions of my job while lost in melancholy. Suddenly gunfire shattered the early morning of Christmas Eve. Three stray bullets hit the wall a few feet from where I was standing but it left me strangely unmoved and unconcerned about the reality of the danger.

It was as if I was frozen in time, standing on the outside looking in. I didn't react to what was happening as nervous customers ran into the bakery for shelter. The shock and numbness gave way sometime later that day, but I cannot say that I experienced fear, panic, or anxiety. I was just getting more depressed that worsened as the day continued. The robber, who was exchanging gun fire with the Brinks Guard in the store, was fatally wounded, he later collapsed and died in the parking lot as he tried to make his way to the get-away car. His body was covered by a sheet but remained there for hours while the store had to open up again and continue with business.

WAAR IS JOU HUIS DAN?

There are times in each person's life when it is the end of one journey, and the beginning of another

I am my history
where I have been
and what I have seen

Part of me is full of excitement
with lessons to learn
and my dreams that yearn

My past and my future
are forever intertwined
to complete my soul
and make my destiny divine

— EMBRACING MY
JOURNEY

Ps 16:11 "You have made known to me the path of life. You will fill me with joy in Your presence."

I never anticipated immigration to be such a continuous and painful experience. Our decision to leave South Africa was devastating for the whole family, for those who left and for those left behind. Shortly after we emigrated my father found my daughter, Nita, sitting outside on the steps, crying uncontrollably. He sat down to comfort her and asked her what had made her so sad. Through her tears she sobbed that she just wanted to return to the family home that was no more.

In Afrikaans "oupa" means grandfather, my children called my father *Oupie Vos*. 'Pierewiet' was my father's nickname for Nita. This poignant moment can best be explained that my father, who was a very wise man who always offered an insightful perspective to every problem in life, answered Nita's problem with a question:

> *Ewe verslae het Oupie Vos gevra: "Maar Pierewiet*
> *waar is jou huis dan?"*
> *(Astounded Oupie Vos asked: "But Pierewiet where is*
> *your home then?")*

I could not foresee that our immigration would divide my family so completely and so permanently for all the years to come.

We made difficult choices but looking at the bigger picture, what we went through brought me to this place where I am in life, and one that has a lot of goodness. If I could describe my life using only a word, it would be "meaningful." The places I have been and the things I have seen created a desire within me to pursue a better tomorrow. My future decisions lie hidden in past experiences and I draw from the past to shape my future.

BY THE GRACE OF GOD

It was early morning on 5 August 2005, when we received an e-mail bearing terrible news form South Africa. Cecil, Nita's husband, sent an urgent message to inform us that they were in a bad car accident. Cecil, Nita, Vincent, and Grenwill were driving on Friday afternoon from Durban to Klerksdorp when a truck hit their car from the side, impacting more the rear of the vehicle than the front. Cecil suffered a few broken ribs, Vincent a broken arm, and Nita had no injuries except some bruises.

Poor little Grenwill, 9-years old at the time, was sitting at the impact point and suffered the worst. His skull was crushed with severe damage to his right ear and the nerves in that area and wasn't breathing when they removed him from the car. The accident took place on a farm road but by the grace of God a doctor who was driving behind the ambulance decided to investigate and arrived at the scene of the accident. His timely arrival and interventions saved Grenwill's life on the side of the road. He then travelled in the ambulance to Kroonpark Hospital, arranging for a Neurosurgeon to meet at the hospital.

Grenwill was rushed into surgery without delay, after which he was placed on life-support then transferred to Bloemfontein Hospital as they were better equipped to care for him. There the doctor told Nita and Cecil that Grenwill would likely be brain dead and bed-bound for the rest of his life. He was in a coma for ten days before he regained consciousness and on the first day, nurses tried to stand him up but his legs couldn't take his weight. It was only then that they discovered he had a fractured femur, the full extent of his injuries revealing themselves over the next few weeks. He stayed in hospital for 3-weeks. The right side of his face was paralyzed, and he became deaf in his right ear, his road to recovery was long, requiring physical therapy and further surgeries.

Over time the paralysis subsided but he never recovered hearing in his right ear. His broken bones healed and surgery restored his face to the point where one could hardly tell that he had suffered injury, but much couldn't be fixed. The driver of the truck was faulted for the accident and after years of legal proceedings a trust was established to provide for Grenwill.

Tomorrow, tomorrow
when will it come
will I forget then
about yesterday's sorrow
Don't wait until tomorrow
to forget past sorrow
Tomorrow will never come
We only have yesterday and today

— TOMORROW

Mt 6:34 "Therefore do not worry about tomorrow, for tomorrow will worry about itself. Each day has enough trouble of its own."

SOUTH AFRICA

Like a rainbow that fades away
because it was never meant to stay
so life events will come and go
as my plans will change and grow

Each time a rainbow falls apart
there will be another journey to start
with new dreams to pursue again
It is my choice what will remain
of the lessons I have learned
and the wisdom that it earned

— *WHEN RAINBOWS FALL*
APART

Job 6:13 "Do I have any power to help myself, now that success has been driven from me?"

My daughter, Nita, was diagnosed with cancer and scheduled for a hysterectomy on 17 February 2014. I do not cope well when my loved ones are facing harm, my heart broke knowing that I could not be with her during that trying time. The surgery went well however, and the surgeon was well pleased with the outcome. Nita was recovering steadily at home and to help with the recovery, Cecil, her husband, took her for evening walks around their neighborhood.

Across the street from their home is a local convenient store owned by friends of theirs. After their evening walk,

Nita watched from their house as Cecil walked across the street and entered the store, walking straight into an armed robbery in progress. Horrified Nita watched as the robber turned towards Cecil and began shooting, dropping Cecil to the ground almost immediately. The owner's son who was tending the store had already alerted his father and within minutes he had arrived, forcing the robbers to quickly flee the scene.

The owner helped Cecil into his car and they pursued the robbers while Nita frantically called Cecil only to discover that he left his phone at home. She was in too much pain from the surgery to do anything else but slowly walk outside as she desperately waited for news. After what must have felt like an eternity, Cecil and the owner of the store returned to her. Cecil's military training had served him well, when he saw the gunman, he dropped to the floor and avoided being shot, his clear mind had saved his life.

Unarmed and unharmed, Cecil and the store owner didn't think twice before chasing after the robbers and were able to get the license plate number of the get-away car. With this information, along with an accurate description of the vehicle and the gunmen, the police were able to locate the robbers and their car within two days. After the ordeal Cecil and Nita were eager to be with their family and as soon as Nita recovered well enough to undertake the journey, they came to visit us in Miami.

GRANDMA DAYS

My twenties came
and with that came…kids
I'm mostly running late
with little patience and energy
but with one comforting thought though
This too shall pass
because forty means freedom
With the kids all grown
and on their own

Then my forties came
so with that came…grandkids
and all of a sudden I have
more of the same
But with one difference though
the lessons that I have learned

Then my sixties came
so with that came…great grandkids
And oh, how I long to have
more of the same
But sadly, it's not meant to be

— MORE OF THE SAME

Pr 17:6 "Children's children are the crown of old men; and the glory of children are their fathers."

. . .

Raising a big family is quite a challenge, my twin boys were 2.4-years old when my twin girls were born, we were only expecting to have three children but quickly had six. Once the kids were all grown and had become parents themselves, they still needed our support and we were fortunate to spend valuable time with our grandchildren. Before I knew it, my grandchildren were grown with kids of their own and separations came that I did not anticipate.

I have learned to live with numerous losses and it's not always the death of a loved one. It is seldom realized how traumatic it can be to leave your homeland, I mourn the loss that I should have been a part of my children's everyday life, to visit at their home and spend time with their children. The ache has never settled within me, despite all this time, I am sad that Nita, Cecil and their boys, Vincent and Grenwill, are in South Africa while we are in Miami. My grandchildren grew into men and we hardly know them or much about their lives. It is doubtful we'll ever get to know our great-grandchildren who were born in South Africa. This continues to bring heartache and will most likely be another loss that I keep within my heart.

Chapter Eight

Y2K AND MINDGAMES

Relationships are like bank accounts, if I keep withdrawing but fail to make deposits, I will end up overdrawn.

LADIES BOOT CAMP

I had the unforgettable experience to attend 'Ladies Boot Camp' where we spent the entire weekend 'camping out' at church whilst engaging in depth studies of the Bible that focused on facing and overcoming our own shortcomings. The first morning during prayer, a picture of a puppy came to my mind, I thought it was just my own wandering mind because why would God show me a puppy? Then a dog in the neighborhood began barking and, in my mind, I saw a picture of a pole and chain. Feeling in my spirit the need to give up whatever tied me down, the 'pole and chain' were of my own making.

The last morning of the Boot Camp I had a picture in my mind of beautiful open plains and horses across them and from that vision I realized that it would be a challenge for me to slay the giants of negative thinking, sloth and apathy. Most of the skeletons in my closet were those of broken relationships, the consequences of being aloof and neglectful, of broken promises and dreams. All the kind acts and good intentions that died there and were never pursued.

Is this really me
I live my life
in shades of mediocrity
I say
I want no strife
and stay
an uninvolved spectator of life

My empty words come back to me
that hollow sound of apathy
I mean it when I say

I promise I will pray
and I do regret
when I so quickly forget
and God must say –
"you know, this is not the way"

I confess my self-righteousness
my fear and my laziness
under achiever, people pleaser –
Lord I need you to guide me
and set me free from apathy

— *THE WATCHER*

Jas 4:17 "Anyone, then who knows the good he ought to do and doesn't do it, sins."

CHANGE

The time has come and now is

> *God came into my closet one day*
> *He took all the skeletons away*
> *and threw it into the deepest sea*
> *Then He said to me: "I will remember it no more"*
>
> *And after a long time*
> *my closet still looked fine*
> *But God said to me one day:*
> *"I know it's true, you have no skeletons there*
> *but my child, your closet is bare.*
> *You have to replace that empty space."*

— *THE CLOSET*

Jer 48:10 "A curse on him who is lax in doing the Lord's work."

As the century nears its end, people started to prepare for 'Y2K', the common term describing a feared technological problem where the coding of computerized systems was written with a 2-digit year, not a 4-digit year, meaning 1900 was indistinguishable from 2000. The original programmers simply didn't think that far ahead, and it was done simply to save space and data. But as we approached the end of the century, panic ensued as experts contemplated what the outcome could be.

The society, heavily dependent on computerized systems did not know how the systems would react if it, in effect, believed that 2000 was 1900. Most predicted that the system would crash because the chronology would not match the operating software. Companies spent millions to upgrade and test new software and fear grew about what might happen at the turn of the century. Some believed nothing would happen, others proclaimed it was the end of life as we knew it. I went to a few meetings on the subject and prepared as if a hurricane was imminent. In the end, 2000 ticked over with no impact on our computers. So, the old century passed and the new century began.

As for me it was also the end of the old and the beginning of the new. On one of my early morning walks one day whilst I was nearing the end of the block, a hysterical young girl jumped up and down in the middle of the road. On the sidewalk was an ambulance with flashing lights, and paramedics were working on a wounded man who was lying on the grass. I didn't try to find out what was going on nor attempt to comfort the girl, I just wanted to get out of there as soon as possible. Later we found out the injured man was a drug dealer who had been in a knife fight with a peer. Shocked at how little I knew about the happenings in my neighborhood and feeling so out of touch, it was impossible not to get involved.

BREAD AND WINE

Jesus is not about the "Law and the Rod" He is about "Bread and Wine"

When I ask God to forgive my sins, I try to recall all the sins I committed, which is where I have it all wrong. It is not just about what I may have done, but also about what I failed to do. I confess my sin not to be condemned, but to be humbled. Sin has more to do with my wrong attitudes and thoughts, and my lack of love and compassion. Jesus told us that He gives us one command only; to love, because on this one commandment hangs the other nine. If we love others, we are not going to harm them in any way.

As I prayed one day, I became aware of Jesus' presence with me. In His hands He held Bread and Wine, not the Law and the Rod.

Jn 8:3 "They said to Jesus, "Teacher this woman was caught in the act of adultery. In the Law, Moses commanded us to stone such woman. Now what do you say?"

Pick up a stone and throw
Any one of you who know
You have no sin

Jesus bent down and write on the ground
But no one was to be found
When He looked up and wanted to know
Tell Me now, where did they all go

Lord, they did not say when they went away
All quietly without a noise
Not one of them raised his voice

— *THE FIRST STONE*

Jn 8:10 "Jesus straightened up and ask her, "Woman, where are they? Has no one condemn you?" "No one Sir" she said. "Then neither do I condemn you" Jesus declared. "Go now and leave your life of sin.""

Growing up and trying to cope with all the losses I experienced, I pulled away from life and remained aloof and uninvolved. As a parent, I was not emotionally available to my kids, but God didn't abandon me to that state. Even as an adult the desire to hide when life becomes difficult is persistent, but God continues to pull me out of isolation and into the light where I can engage with humanity.

We don't all grieve the same and we are not all touched by grief in the same way. In the passing of time and recovering from the damage that grief brought me, I find myself seeking more strength from my faith in God. Slowly but surely changes began to happen as I become more involved with my family, fellow believers, and community activities. Some of my loved ones drifted away from God and I don't know what else to do except pray.

DISTANCE MAKES NO DIFFERENCE

I met an unusual lady today
and as she walked away
gave me the key to her door
but now she's not around anymore
since she quickly changed the lock
I realize there's something I forgot

This was just an empty promise

Some people never offer more
and won't invite you to their door
they'll make plans like before
but there's nothing to explore
as empty words filled empty space
and plans were made that didn't take place

Friendship needs time to grow
and this is how I will know
when true colors begin so show
if this is really the start
of a bond straight from the heart

— *TRUE COLORS*

Ecc 4:9 "Two are better than one because they have a good return for their work: if one falls down, his friend can help him up, but pity the man who falls and has no one to help him up!"

.   .   .

It was a challenge to learn about friendship this late in my life and I soon realized the importance of paying attention when people showed me their true colors. This helped me understand what to expect from them in the future and not to take all their excuses and justifications so seriously. One lesson my life has taught me is how to walk away and leave problematic situations behind.

Some relationships remain superficial and don't mature into a meaningful connection, that magic ingredient is missing and they will remain just an acquaintance. There might be the occasional lunch with someone who shares mutual interests or occupations, but get-togethers will remain casual in those specific social settings where personal circumstances and opinions might never enter into the conversations.

Then there is that special friendship that goes straight to the heart, where you share similar beliefs and values and there can be transparency in discussions about politics, spirituality, and life choices. Differences can be appreciated and accepted without being judgmental. This is an "A" relationship where I can find Affection, Acceptance, and Appreciation.

RELATIONSHIPS

Relationships are like bank accounts. If I keep withdrawing but don't make any deposits, I will end up overdrawn and I don't want that to happen

There's a story I heard long ago; it happened on a very cold winter's morning, the cows were grazing in the field after they had been milked and there was a small bird that followed them, hoping to get a worm or two in the loose ground. Suddenly a huge heap of cow dung landed right on the bird who started to yell and struggle to get out of the dung. There was a hawk up in the sky and the commotion on the ground attracted his attention, he swooped down and the bird became his breakfast.

The moral of the story is this; in the heat of the moment, it is better to keep quiet, even though you feel you're being dumped on. From there on, it can only go from bad to worse. At times it is necessary to lose an argument to save a relationship and by doing so it will prevent innocent people getting hurt.

This reminds me of an old African saying: "*When the elephants fight, the grass gets trampled.*"

Jas 4:2 "What causes fights and quarrels among you? Don't they come from your desires that battle within you. You want something but don't get it. You kill and covet, but you cannot have what you want. You quarrel and fight. You do not have because you do not ask God. "

I meet friends at the places I go
at church, at work, or school
I meet some for lunch
and others at the pool

But then there are friends
Who will give me their time
During the dark days
they tell me I'll be fine

With friends like that I want to grow old
But they are rare as rubies, precious as gold
and I have been blessed beyond measure
to have found friends who are such a treasure

But even if I have no-one to call friend, Jesus is still
    with me.

— *FRIENDS*

Pr 18:24 "There is a Friend who sticks closer than a brother."

TOTAL CONFUSION

We made happy memories today
so, that we can have them tomorrow
As this time, will surely pass away
and I will remember in times of sorrow
the pleasant memories we made before
and will be encouraged to make even more.

— *HAPPY MEMORIES*

Eph 4:26 "In your anger, do not sin; do not let the sun go down while you are still angry."

Just after my granddaughter Katelyn's third birthday, her mother left leaving my son, Mick, with three children to raise by himself. He moved back in with us for a while to get help with the kids. When they first moved in, I told the kids that nobody in this house would fight with them or yell at them because we don't fight with each other. Matthew, 4-years old at the time, wanted to make sure he understood everything correctly and asked: "but Grandma if we take it outside can we fight then?" Needless to say, I was left speechless.

My grandson Cameron, about 8-years old at the time, came into my room one evening. I put down the book that I was reading to give him my attention, no sooner did he walk in when his face turned pale with fright and he rushed out of the room. The breeze from the ceiling fan was slowly turning the pages of my book, one by one but Cameron hadn't noticed the ceiling fan, he only saw the pages turning all by themselves. He was watching Ghostbusters and was still in the mindset of the movie, he reacted instantly much to our amusement.

During this time my son Duncan and his wife's marriage began falling apart, the demands of police work proved to be too much for her. After they finalized their divorce Duncan too, moved back home with us. At the same time my son-in-law, Randy, began traveling to Georgia for work, my daughter Angie and her baby Abby, also moved in with us. Over weekends, when Randy was in town, his daughter Lindsay (from a previous marriage) also visited with us, leaving us with a full house. When everybody was home, we were eleven family members living in my four-bedroom, three-bathroom home. We used boxes packed with personal belongings to build a wall so we could have an extra room.

Eventually, Angie and Randy moved to Ellijay, in Georgia. It was months after Jeanette's little girl, Lienie, was born before Angie could come home to visit. Angie and Jeanette look so alike it confused Lienie, she was 11-months old when she first saw Angie. That was total confusion. Lienie desperately tried to hold on to both of them and didn't want one of them to leave. She was too young to understand the concept of twins and it took her quite a while to accept the thought that her mom and Angie were twins but she gradually accepted it and named Angie "Mommy Angie."

THE TRADING POST

I love you, not because you're pretty. I love you, not because you're smart. I love you because…you tip-toed into my heart

All the little games you play
and all the silly things you say
Just makes me love you more

With all my things out of place
and playful mischief on your face
It just makes me love you more

I enjoy your giggles and laughter
and I don't think about what may come after
So, for now, I will focus on what matters
I will just love you more

FOR NOW

1 Co 13:1-13 "Love: "Now I will show you the most excellent way"

As the grandmother, Cameron, Matthew, and Katelyn spent their days with me while Mick worked. Grocery shopping with children is always a big challenge, especially shopping with three. It required a little planning and finesse and so we created a plan where we turned shopping into a game with a responsibility for each of the kids.

Katelyn, the 3-year-old, would sit in the shopping cart with my purse and she was assigned the title "The Guardian of the Purse", an important position because without money we couldn't get our supplies, and she knew this. Matthew, the 5-year-old, was assigned the title "The Guardian of Supplies", we needed a strong guy to protect the supplies that we came to get. Lastly, Cameron, the 8-year-old, was "The Scout", he was old enough to find the needed supplies and bring it to the team. And so, grocery shopping became important "excursions to the trading post."

During 2007 a short-lived family tradition started, we came together Tuesday evenings and enjoyed a big dinner. Duncan was off work and would always be home, and everyone else came too. Tuesday night became family night and it was perfect, we had fun, joking, sharing stories, and the kids all played together. One popular game was when I hid in the kitchen and my 2-year-old granddaughter, Lienie, would search for me. She was nervous that I would scare her as she approached the kitchen so I'd stick my foot out the door for her to see, then I'd start tapping it to signal that I was waiting for her. She would shriek and point in anticipation at the sight of my foot and couldn't stop laughing.

After a few years this family tradition sadly came to an abrupt end in 2010.

Chapter Nine

MY YEAR OF MOURNING

I make misfortune work for me. I may bow down but not in defeat.

THE QUESTION OF FAITH

What are your feelings about divine healings?
Some don't believe the claims
while others fake claims for fame
and lie about health and wealth

So we live our lives of pride
with lies that's so easy to hide
and claim from God the power
as people gather around in awe

The speaker shouts to everyone
"Just believe and your will shall be done"
Is there not something that is missed
what about God's will in all this?

We have done it all the same
but God gets the blame.
When lives of lies start falling down
we cannot look at God and frown

         — SO CONFUSED

Pr 19:3 "A man's own folly ruins his life, yet his heart rages against the Lord."

My step-granddaughter, Lindsay, was diagnosed with cancer early in 2009, she was 17-years old and had just graduated from high school. The diagnoses changed over time, beginning with breast cancer, then to other types, and finally ended on Non-Hodgkin's Lymphoma. Every possible treatment was done; chemotherapy, radiation therapy, and finally, a bone marrow transplant. She fought for almost two years but by the beginning of 2010, her doctors sent her home to die.

She was never willing to give up and accept the fact that her time was running out, nor would she consider any final arrangements, her desperate struggle was very hard to witness. It was a Sunday evening in April 2010, when we visited her at Baptist Hospital, that was the last time we saw her alive. She was happy and looked beautiful, she talked about coming home and thanked us for making a room available to her. Her last words to me were: "Just until I'm back on my feet."

That Monday by lunchtime, we got the call that she had passed away. She suddenly started having difficulty breathing, and the nurses incubated her to help her breathe. They asked her if she was okay and she gave them a thumbs-up, just as suddenly her eyes closed and she was gone. We prayed and believed that Lindsay would live but in the end it didn't happen.

LITTLE DID I KNOW

My son held me in his embrace
Wiped the tears from my face

Don't cry mommy
Don't be sad
We are all together
A reason to be glad

Little did I know then
He will be the next to go

Don't cry mommy
Don't be sad

Just say goodbye
That's all I had

— DON'T CRY
MOMMY

1 Th 4:13 "We do not want you to be ignorant about those who fall asleep, or to grieve like the rest of men, who have no hope."

While we were still coping with the death of Lindsay, we were hit with a sudden and unexpected death. On Tuesday, 10 August, my son-in-law Randy (Lindsay and Abby's dad) died in a car accident while on his way to work. Abby, 6-years old at the time, was with him. He lost control of his truck and hit a tree; the truck was so badly damaged the rescue personnel had to cut the roof open to get them out. Abby miraculously was unharmed but was taken via ambulance to the emergency room for a complete evaluation and was kept overnight as a precaution. Pictures of the vehicle showed it was only the section where Abby sat that was intact, the rest of the truck was crushed. She was not seriously injured but severely traumatized and simply pretended that the accident did not occur, she never spoke about it and took a long time to recover.

My son Duncan, left immediately for Georgia as soon as he got the news. He drove all day and arrived that night while Angie was still at the hospital with Abby. Duncan's best friend and fellow police officer, Oscar flew in the next day while I got on the first available flight. Jeanette and Carsten drove up to Georgia with Lienie and Markus, Mick and Cameron arrived shortly thereafter.

Later Abby told her mom: "I'm afraid if anything happens to you there will be no one to care for me." to which her mom assured her that would never happen, and her uncle Duncan was on his way to immediately come get her.

We never imagined what was to follow; one month later, on 18 September, Duncan was in a serious car accident, he was driving home late at night and, exhausted, he fell asleep behind the wheel and hit a tree.

10/7

In this desert of grief
one finds no relief
as one thirsts for peace
from pain that won't cease

God will ease my soul
and make rivers flow
He will change this desert of grief
and tomorrow my heart will be free…

DESERT OF GRIEF

Isa 43:19 "I am making a way in the desert, and streams in the wasteland."

Very early in the morning Oscar came to tell us that Duncan was in a serious car accident and was taken to Jackson Memorial Hospital. Duncan had many friends who showed their support but the prognosis was not good. The doctors worked hard to save him, he had broken bones, internal damage, and was on life-support.

My daughter Nita in South Africa made travel arrangements as soon as she heard the news and was in Miami a few days later, knowing the emotional turmoil that we were in. She had been there, years ago when her family was in a terrible accident and my grandson, Grenwill, was on life support. Her strong, bubbly personality charmed all those around her and gave us all the strength we could find nowhere else. Thank you, Nita we will always value this time we had together.

During Duncan's hospital stay, my daughter Jeanette, took over most of the interactions with the hospital staff. She is the nurse in the family and thus was best qualified to handle these matters. Duncan suffered brain injuries, developed pneumonia, his kidneys were bleeding and couldn't work fluids out of his body. The result was large scale swelling that created huge blisters on his arms and legs, committing him to life support for three weeks. The doctors worked tirelessly and did all they could, but in the end, we were left with the difficult decision to continue breathing assistance or to discontinue. Duncan was taken off life support and as he was, I lifted my hands up to God and said, "Father I give him into Your hands", as soon as I released him to God's care peace came over me and calmed my troubled mind.

He was taken off life support on 6 October, and miraculously he started to breath on his own. We all released a stressful sigh of relief, his two sisters, Nita and Angie, waited with him but his breathing grew shallower during the night. Jeanette came the next morning to be with Duncan so Nita and Angie could get some rest. During one of these 'shift changes' whilst no one was in the room, he stopped breathing, when Jeanette walked back into the room he was already gone. At shift-change he called in his 10/7, which means in police language: "End of Watch."

PAINFUL THOUGHTS

Negative voices in my head
shout so loud I cannot hear
the gentle voice of reason
pleading to be listened to
but to no avail
The dark shadows looming
appear to be
more than a match for me

— *VOICE OF*
REASON

Ps 55:6 "I said, Oh, that I had the wings of a dove! I would fly away and be at rest."

The police arranged a procession with a limousine to pick us up at home and took us to Stanfill Funeral Home where Duncan's last journey started. The procession went on for miles and miles, a significant portion of the main highway in our area (US1) was blocked off and people got out of their cars and saluted us. The support we received from the Miami-Dade Police Department was unwavering. The police counselor, Melissa Barosela, was available to all of us who needed her help and made the first Christmas without Duncan bearable with her graceful presence, understanding, and compassion.

The morning of the funeral, my granddaughter Elina, was very excited when she got into the limousine and told us this would be her first "limbo ride." She didn't know then where we were going and her smiles soon changed to tears when she realized. She loved Duncan and so did her little brother Markus, but he was still too young to understand the ramifications of the loss, and the funeral. Duncan invested a lot of time into his family and was well loved by every one of us. When we arrived at the church it seemed as if the entire police department were there, and many spoke to memorialize Duncan, including Director James K Loftus and Oscar. Angie delivered the eulogy on behalf of the family. Afterwards, we gathered at Duncan's home where many people came to share their fond memories of Duncan with us.

At times my thoughts feel like a heap of marbles in the middle of a floor, then suddenly, a heavy object smashes into the marbles and they scatter uncontrollably in all directions and I am unable to keep myself together. Sometimes I would question why God allows so much pain in my life. Struggling to get through the long hard day, I tried to alleviate the pain a little by thinking about happier times.

I was watching Elina, my granddaughter, she is named after my sister but she's quite the opposite, a spirited little girl and always the center of attention. My mind went back to a day at the Miami Aquarium. She was about 3-years old and doing her little dance on the stage and so didn't notice that the dolphins had entered the pool behind her. As the audience stood and began clapping, she thought they were clapping in appreciation of her dancing, leaving her feeling mighty pleased with herself.

DESERT DEMONS

I have in my memory
the reflection of a mystery
In color and evasiveness
lies its own attractiveness
But it is such a mystery

The devil comes with pretty illusions
Too late we make the right conclusions
He will show us the reflection
and make us believe in the perfection
He leads us with pervasiveness
and shows us the attractiveness
But it is only an illusion

— ILLUSIONS

1 Pe 5:8 "Be self-controlled and alert. Your enemy the devil prowls
around like a roaring lion, looking for someone to devour."

A person in pain is vulnerable, unable to concentrate, think, or rest. Exhausted, grief-stricken people make poor decisions. Frustrated with myself, I can see my vulnerability but I am in too much pain to do much about it. Death has the power to hurt deeply and while in that wounded state the devil doesn't come to me with an obvious weapon. Rather, he comes to me with a velvet glove and soothing words to put my mind at ease. Dying in the desert of thirst and exhaustion, I see an oasis, but I know the water will be bitter and won't nourish me, but the oasis puts my mind in a tranquil place and numbs the pain of the desert's empty nothingness. I don't have the emotional strength to fight those desert demons, the cool restfulness of the oasis is such a welcoming place, but I have learned that if I stay in that illusion too long it can be devastating. Negative ways to cope with pain will only open up a whole new world of misery.

My 'needs' may cost me more than what I can afford to pay. What am I willing to sacrifice that will satisfy my needs and find relief from the awful pain? A quick fix will wear off just as quickly, but the consequences will linger. Many defenses will numb one's pain and offer an escape, but in life there is always a price to pay. I needed to break free of those hurtful thought patterns and develop healing ones. To help me in my effort to recover, I decided to go back to school, knowing that having a goal to work towards would create some of the positivity that I needed.

I trained through the University Baptist Church to become a Stephen Minister, which focused on one-on-one care and helping techniques. These courses were enlightening to me and through my efforts to try and help others I found that I helped myself. Most interesting to me were the classes on Temperament Studies, a process that makes sense to me. Like recipes for a spicy meal or sweet desert, some ingredients naturally belong together, likewise I saw that certain temperament traits naturally belong together, extrovert or introvert. In all the confusion that life had churned up for me, it was good to find some common sense.

DON'T SMOKE THAT STUFF

I can compare bereavement to being lost in a dark forest rife with snakes, spiders, and hidden pitfalls, while listening to the howling of night creatures. I'm groping around, trying to find my way, but in the darkness, I am lost and I don't know if I am going in circles or finding my way out. But eventually daybreak came and I felt more sure-footed. One day I realized the sun was beginning to shine through again and a new day was dawning.

Lost in a dark and forlorn place
On a soul-wrenching journey
And the winding road
is thorny and narrow
If only I can find some relief

My heart is so painfully empty
it yearns for that feeling
of togetherness, endlessly
Like songs longing to be sung
But the voice is gone
Search as I may – I find nothing…

— LOST

1 Pe 5:7 "Cast all your anxiety on Him because he cares for you."

Grieving is an unstable process where most days can be horribly painful and other days aren't as bad, and occasionally a day that is quite good. The good days are enjoyed with the bitter longing for it not to end. One morning, feeling particularly good, with some sense of well-being, I said to my manager at the bakery: "You know Jorge, bad things happen but life is good." He looked at me in amazement and jokingly replied: "Elizabeth you need to stop smoking that stuff. You cannot keep on doing that."

Grieving is painful in many ways and sets off a cascading effect in all aspects of your life. One doesn't simply deal with the pain of a loss but watches their entire life fall apart while fighting to keep it together. With all the time being absent from work to deal with all the tragedies, I fell behind on my annual hour requirements to keep my insurance benefits. The end of the year was fast approaching and finding ways to make up my lost hours became almost impossible. Jorge went above and beyond to help me in that respect, he called other locations and found spots for me to fill. If the alternate locations were too far away, he would drive me there and picked me up after my shift.

Thanks to Jorge I was able to work enough hours to keep my insurance. He showed deep understanding and compassion, he patiently listened to me and sometimes suggested another way to look at the situation. He made many bad days so much better and I affectionately referred to him as "Dr. Jorge." When you lose a loved one you can recognize some of their characteristics in someone else. I saw some of Duncan in Jorge.

HEARTBREAK AT DAYBREAK

Duncan was about 11-years old when I forgot to pick him up from school one day. I still thank God that the principal went back to school that afternoon around 5 o'clock. While busy preparing supper a very upset principal called to let me know that Duncan was still at school, an incident I will never forget. At times bringing it up in conversations with Duncan, I would tell him how bad I felt about it and how truly sorry I was, to which he would very graciously tell me: "it is no big deal."

After Duncan passed away this memory bothered me a lot. Was he so insignificant that I couldn't even remember to pick him up when he was finished with his after-school activities? Working through my grief, one of my assignments from Dr. Teddy was to go back to the place of the accident, just around the corner from our home and promise Duncan that I will never again forget him and to write a poem about the accident.

Since you hit that tree
just around the corner
that took you so far away from me
I became your mourner

Just a few blocks from home
we passed by your car
with your blood on the street
The darkness mercifully hid
what's left of your tragedy

It was the breaking of day
and I began to pray
as pain overwhelms me

and I'm unable to speak

Words cannot describe you
Your deeds were honest and true
I will never forget you
From now until eternity

— *JUST AROUND THE*
CORNER

Ps 42:11 "Why are you in despair, O my soul? And why have you become disturbed within me? Hope in God, for I shall yet praise Him, the help of my countenance and my God."

THE LINKING OBJECT

While Duncan was staying with us, he always kept his bedroom door locked as being a police officer, his guns needed to be securely out of reach from the others in the house. In January of 2010 he bought a house close to us and when he moved out, he left his bedroom key on the mirror in the hallway. There was no reason to take the key down, but after Duncan passed away, I became very aware of the key. Walking past the mirror I would look at the key and touch it but could not take it down. Then after a long time, I first took a picture of the key and after that I had enough courage to take it off the mirror.

In my next counseling session, I wrapped the key in soft paper, sealed it in a zip lock bag and took it with me. Now I keep his old bedroom key on my keychain, in my mind it remained Duncan's key to Duncan's room. My next challenge from Dr. Teddy was to change the way I looked at Duncan's room and to give his room a new name and a new, good purpose. Continuing in Duncan's spirit of goodness, his old room became my study and the key is my linking-object.

I remember when Duncan left his key there
after he emptied the room of his belongings
This is so hard, it's just not fair
what do I do with my longings

What can I do and where can I start
to find the key that unlocks my heart
with memories that will set me free
and bring back the whole world to me

When my agony rejects

the memories I protect
his key is the linking object
to keep it all intact

But it wasn't easy to reclaim
a room haunted by love and pain
It took me a while to understand
I need to keep Duncan's key in my hand

I will no longer lock him out
I will rather lock him in.

— THE KEY

Isa 41:10 "Fear not, for I am with you; be not dismayed, for I am your God. I will strengthen you, Yes, I will help you, I will uphold you with My Righteous right hand."

OFFICER DUNCAN KIDSON FOOD PANTRY

In May of 2011, Bay Community Church opened "The Officer Duncan Kidson Food Pantry". The picture of Duncan with the turtle that he rescued from the traffic, became the logo for the food pantry. Duncan was truly here to serve and to protect and we are pleased the food pantry was named after him, he would have liked that a lot.

Duncan loved to eat; every day I called to tell him what I was preparing for dinner and invited him to join us, his friends were also welcome. At times, he would come into the kitchen, put his arm around me and jokingly say: "Woman, where's the food!" After he passed away, I struggled to get back into the kitchen to prepare a meal. We had a picture of Duncan on the kitchen table, so we added a balloon with his name on it to celebrate his life and remember all the happy times we shared together.

With the help of a member from Bay Community Church, Magic City Casino supported the Food Pantry and in April of 2013 we received a check from Magic City Casino for three-thousand six hundred dollars in support of the Food Pantry. In December of 2013 we received another check from Magic City Casino for eight-thousand dollars, also in support of the food pantry. There was an article of the donation in The Miami Herald on 19 January 2014.

I see your face
In the shadows on the wall
But when I call your name,
silence echoes back at me

Talking to myself
I remember

how I use to be
...me

Now I am not the same
I am broken
and it will take time
to see the shattered pieces
take on new shapes
...in me

This loss has changed me in every way
I will be different....
Better...to become and be
A stronger and wiser me...

                — SHADOWS

Jas 5:16 "The prayer of the righteous is powerful and effective."

BADGE OF HOPE

I make misfortune work for me. I may bow down but not in defeat

> *Why do I survive this life with all its sorrow?*
> *Have I done someone wrong somewhere?*
> *I don't know where*
> *No, I don't know where*
>
> *I didn't look for these opportunities*
> *But what was right came to me*
> *This is whom I am to be*
> *If not so – I cannot be*
>
> — *SEARCH FOR MEANING*

Ps 91:15 "He will call upon Me, and I will answer him; I will be with him in trouble, I will deliver him and honor him."

I enrolled in a training program through Baptist Health Systems Bereavement Support to become a bereavement facilitator which was a continuous series of classes designed to teach volunteers to help the bereaved. Duncan passed away 7 October 2010. My first class was 7 October 2011 at the Crossroads Counseling Center with psychologist Dr. Teddy Tarr. As I entered her office, I saw ornamental turtles everywhere, it was as if Duncan had blessed my decision and agreed that I was in the right place. I didn't think it was the right time to do this training, but in my mind, I saw how Duncan always stood tall and strong when a difficult task had to be completed and punched with his fist into the palm of his open hand and say: "This is game time." With that attitude I pursued my training and completed all the qualifications.

I believe in support groups; they provide a bridge over troubled water for those who need it. Police Officers, Melissa Barosela and DeiDei Beecher, invited me to join them in their plans to create "Badge of Hope", a bereavement support group for police officers and their families. We also started a bereavement group through Bay Community Church with the help of my pastor, John Churchill. I cannot choose what life brings me; I can only choose how I respond. In my brokenness God can use me as a wounded healer and so bring healing to others. I believe God called me to this mission and it has helped me manage my own losses. I will wait in the hallway and when God opens the door, I will walk through.

I can compare grief to a dark alley in a bad neighborhood, late at night. It is a scary place to be alone, but in the company of others it is not as bad anymore. In support groups we are not alone in our grief, but in the company of people who understand the loss and pain as they face similar struggles. We are all so uniquely different and each of us respond in our own way. Even after all I have been through, I cannot say to anyone "I know how you feel", but I know the depth of those emotions and the enormity of the loss.

ALL BY MYSELF

I don't like to be home alone or to go out on my own, feeling insecure, it's difficult to trust my own abilities. I don't like to drive, not because I fear getting into a car accident, but I'm afraid I'll get lost. If I find myself in the wrong lane and cannot make the right turn, it will be difficult to find my way back. I'm afraid the car will break down and I will be stranded on my own, especially at night. Feeling vulnerable makes me shy away from challenges, so resistance became entrenched in my mind. This intensified after my sister, who lived in South Africa, was attacked in her home by three armed men.

I have never lived through a decade without suffering some untimely loss. It helped me to cope with all these accumulated losses when I become involved with support groups. That is how a scary but exciting challenge presented itself to me through Badge of Hope, the police bereavement group. It was located in an area far from my home which meant I would have to find my way there and back, all by myself, at night. My daughter accompanied me on a few trial runs while I made notes and wrote down landmarks. It's a long distance from where we live, with traveling time being about one hour. Then the big evening came.

It was awesome to make it all the way to Doral where the meeting was taking place, without getting myself into a state of panic. Shaking like a leaf in the wind I called my family to tell them that I had arrived safely. But there was even a bigger challenge to face on my return journey. It was dark by then and almost impossible to recognize most of the landmarks I had memorized and follow my directions home and using "Waze" all the way home with more than an hour of traveling time might drain the phone battery, a risk I didn't want to take. I prayed all the way there and back and it felt really good finally arrive home safely.

> *My brain cannot retain*
> *What you try to explain*
> *So please be patient*
> *My brain is ancient*
> *But not complacent*
>
> *Until the day I die*
> *I will always try to learn*
> *and not just to get by*
>
> *On my last day with you*
> *when my life is through*
> *you will find,*
> *to this I always tried to be true*
>
> — *LEARNING*

2 Tim 1:7 "For God did not give us a spirit of timidity but a spirit of power, of love, and of self-discipline."

Chapter Ten

MY TOOLBOX

Like butterflies pollinate flowers, so special people come into my life to bring me new hope for the future.

ELIZABETH KIDSON

MY TOOL BOX

My toolbox was always full of stuff I thought might be useful, leaving it full to the brim of a range of tools. Eventually the time came to reconsider their worth, get rid of some old tools, and choose different ones that will better help me manage life. Gratitude has helped me through many difficult times, feeling immensely grateful for the support I get from the loving people in my life. Like butterflies pollinate flowers, they come into my life to bring new hope for the future. This softened the hardship and sorrow that came my way. I started journaling when we came to America, it started off small with a few random poems and reflections, but it became more intense with time, helping me to remember all the extraordinarily events that shaped my life.

I read a psychological study that found people who struggle with painful memories get great relief if they can forgive. Follow-up tests showed that they forgot the details of the forgiven offense while those who couldn't forgive continued to be haunted by the painful details. Forgiving someone is what I do for myself, for my peace of mind and my healing. We cannot forget what happened in the past but the memories lose the power to hurt us. It is a process and takes time, but when I became willing, God put forgiveness in my heart and the result was truly a miracle. The pain and anger dissipate before the Son of God, like mist vanishes before the sun.

When life gets rough, one of my coping strategies has always been to pursue a new hobby, it's like a tool in my toolbox. Before we immigrated, I took classes to make stained glass ornaments and gave those to my family before we came to Miami. I enjoy being creative and find great pleasure in the hobbies I pursue. One I couldn't master was playing the guitar, but I still enjoy playing and singing when nobody is around.

If I could have
told you what I know
I would have,
a long time ago

I carried this heavy load
on a deceitful slippery road
only to turn back the time
could ease this burden of mine

But it is only now that I know
and that I begin to understand
that I have to take this heavy load
and put it all in God's hands

— *HEAVY LOADS ON SLIPPERY*
ROADS

Col 3:13 "Bear with each other, forgive whatever grievance you. have against one another. Forgive as the Lord forgave you."

YOUR BRAIN ON CRAFTING

There are ancient pathways in my mind
that has been ingrained
since the beginning of my time
These familiar pathways
are what my memory is made of
Mental places I revert back to
during times of trouble

These emotional triggers
have powerful urges
that take me to places
I don't want to be

As I struggle to find better ways
I build new pathways in my mind
But in times of trouble
it is so easy to find my way back
to the familiar paths I know
that lead to places hard to go

— *ANCIENT PATHWAYS*

Isa 64:8 "O Lord, you are our Father. We are the clay, You are the potter. We are all the work of Your Hands."

I always had the privilege to be creative and can see God's hand in my work history and how He provided careers to work out in my best interest. I enjoyed both my career choices and my hobbies. A new hobby puts me in a different frame of mind but I never understood why at the time. I had to brace myself going through many storms, but never realized the important role my career and hobbies played in my overall well-being. A recent study titled "This is your brain on Crafting" explains why being creative is so enjoyable and has such great physical benefit. When you do something pleasurable the reward center in your brain releases a neurotransmitter called dopamine which in itself is a natural anti-depressant. Crafting helps with anxiety, depression, and chronic pain.

After Hurricane Andrew in 1992, I took pottery classes and found it to be more than a hobby, I identified strongly with the Biblical concept of myself as a lump of clay in God's hands where He lovingly holds me and molds me. He will make me beautiful and useful. During this time, I needed God's personal touch, to be held in His hands and to be shaped according to His plan, to guard my thoughts and renew my mind. It's a constant and difficult process, many times I'll slide back into old destructive ways of thinking, but thanks to God, He doesn't leave me there.

I recently read an article "This is your brain on Crafting" by Jacque Wilson (CNN) which explains why being creative is so enjoyable and has such great benefits.

"Crafting helps those who suffer from anxiety, depression, or chronic pain. It can ease stress, increase happiness and protect the brain from damage caused by aging. Similar to the mental health benefits of meditation. Whatever form of creating – music, knitting, quilting, tapestry, cake decorating – is beneficial in a number of important ways. It has effects similar to medication. You can be so completely absorbed by an activity that nothing else seems to matter – that's the secret to happiness. Our

nervous system can process only a certain amount of information at a time. That is why we cannot understand two people who are talking to us at the same time. With creativity our existence outside that activity becomes "temporarily suspended." There is not enough attention left over to monitor how the body feels – being hungry or tired.

"The effects of creativity are similar to those of meditation and can reduce stress and fight inflammation. Our bodies are in a constant state of stress and the brain cannot tell the difference between a life-threatening situation or a merely stressful one. The repetitive motions of a creative activity, like knitting, activates the parasympathetic nervous system which quiets the 'flight or fight' response. People can use creative activities as a non-pharmaceutical way to regulate strong emotions and prevent irrational thoughts.

"When you do something pleasurable the reward center in your brain release a neurotransmitter called dopamine. In and of itself dopamine is a natural anti-depressant and any time we can find a non-medicinal way to stimulate the reward center, the better off we will be. Depressed people usually feel better after knitting, the rewards for being creative goes beyond the creation itself. To see the finished creation or to receive praise from a loved one, offer repeated hits of the feel-good chemical. Crafting improves our self-efficacy, which is key to how we approach new challenges, overcome irrational thoughts, and dampen internal chaos.

"Research show that our brains are flexible and can adapt to their environment even in old age, a concept called neuroplasticity, intellectually stimulating activities like learning a new language can help prevent cerebral atrophy and decline in dementia. Creating is unique in its ability to involve many different areas of the brain, it can work your memory and

attention span while involving your visuospatial processing, creative side, and problem-solving abilities."

Ro 8:28 "We know that in all things God works for the good or those who love Him."

STAINED GLASS

How can being broken have a purpose?
Stained glass art
starts with broken pieces
broken but not worthless

Each piece has a purpose
a place where it belongs
with a plan to complete
and a goal to achieve

The end result will be
admired for its exquisite beauty
and value beyond compare

But it had to be broken pieces
before it could fit anywhere

— *BROKEN*

I need a place to belong, and a goal to achieve in order to feel well. I need people who will hold me close, and act in my best interest. I look at my life and see all the broken pieces but have no idea how it will ever come together in complete wholeness. Only God can put all these broken pieces together in a meaningful way with a magnificent end result. But lots of the pieces will not fit into God's plan and will have to be released, which is the beauty of being broken. All the wrong thoughts and attitudes that bring only confusion and poor decisions will have to be chipped away.

Everything I go through in this life is to prepare me for eternity. I don't know how I can face life without leaning on Jesus Christ every day, every step of the way. I agree with those who say Christianity is a crutch. The day I die, when I sigh my last sigh and there is nothing beyond this life, I won't lose anything. So, it doesn't really matter if I'm wrong, I won't even know that. I will have exactly the same as all others who believe there is nothing else, but what we have in this life. Believing in eternal life makes my life here bearable and gives me the strength to go on, knowing that I will be reunited with my loved ones again in paradise.

Ps 23:6 "Surely goodness and love will follow me all the days of my life, and I will dwell in the house of the Lord forever."

NOBODY IS PROMISED TOMORROW

Thinking of all my losses, I'm reminded of the Japanese concept of "kintsukuroi" which means "golden repair" and refers to the potter's art of restoring fractured pots with gold. This practice celebrates imperfections as beautiful and important by illuminating it with gold, literally. The damage is considered something not to be disguised, but to celebrate as a meaningful part of the spirit. In kintsukuroi, true life begins the moment something breaks and reveals its vulnerability.

> *My old heart, broken in million pieces*
> *has been mended with gold*
> *The fractures illuminate*
> *the beauty of a new being*
> *as the grace of God shines through me*
>
> — *SCARRED HEART*

2 Co 6:2 "I tell you, now is the time of God's favor, now is the day of salvation."

My son Laurence was killed on 30 April 1991, even now that date still brings me sadness. Remembering how–for both my twin sons–there was a day when they left home and never came back, a moment when I knew we could never talk to them again. This truth haunted me that afternoon while writing a speech for the Officer Duncan Kidson Food Pantry. My theme that evening was 'Nobody is Promised Tomorrow', my intended message was to encourage everyone to think about where they will spend eternity and to accept Jesus if they haven't already done so. Life will always bring rough weather but if you build your house on rock you will prevail, those who build their homes on sand may go under when the storm hits. That evening after my speech was done, many people came for prayer and counseling, the evening turned out to be a painfully prophetic moment.

At the time, while preparing this speech, my sister Lien, was attacked when her home was invaded in South Africa. While I was delivering my speech she was already gone, I just didn't know it yet. Lien was hosting a Bible Study group when three armed men entered her home. It was 27 April 2016; the security gate was unlocked and her husband was in Mozambique for his work. This home invasion was well planned, the robbers knew about the security cameras and that there was a gun safe. One of them held up the guests, one searched the house for valuables, and one took my sister to unlock the safe. She could not get it open, so he hit her, she died on her way to the hospital. The robbers took my sister's car, her purse, the security system, and other electronics. The police did a superficial investigation and mentioned that there were five robberies in the neighborhood that evening. They suspected that the thieves drove the cars with stolen goods over the border into Swaziland and simply disappeared.

Early Thursday morning, 28 April, we started getting messages from Vincent in South Africa, they were desperately trying to reach us to talk about the tragedy that had just struck.

FORGIVENESS

Forgiveness and gratitude are powerful weapons

Durban, South Africa
Wednesday evening, 27 April 2016

It's unbearable to think that Elina's last moments where steeped in fear and violence, thinking of the desperate fear and anxiety she must have endured, was too much for me. Then I heard from her Bible Buddies what her last moments was like; she didn't freak out or beg and plead, she began to pray and lost consciousness with a prayer on her lips. I thank God she had her Bible group with her when she was attacked, she was not alone.

As Christians, we encounter daily struggles, but God can change my outlook on life and I will begin to feel different about my situation. This brings me to forgiveness, it's what I do for myself, for my peace of mind, and my healing. Psychological Studies proved that people who struggle with painful memories of an offence against them find great relief if they can forgive. Bad memories of a tormented mind, the anger and pain, start to vanish.

God gave us a memory for our own protection and to keep us out of harm's way. I didn't forget about the past, I cannot forget that my son was murdered, and I cannot forget that my sister was murdered, but the memories lost their power to torture me. They can no longer hold me prisoner in that dark dungeon, I am free. I no longer think about my sister as being attacked in her home; I think about her on the motorcycle cruising up the coast with her 'Bikers for Christ' friends. That's the picture I have of her in my mind and in my living room, that's the way I remember her.

I will pay a high price.
if my heart remains cold as ice
and I just cannot start
changes that will warm my heart

through compassion I get involved
and so are problems solved
to become aware of the needs
but not neglect the deeds

— *COLD AS ICE*

Lk 9:62 "Jesus replied, "No-one who puts his hand to the plough and looks back is fit for service in the kingdom of God.""

THE GLASS WALL

To my sister Elina

Imagine if nobody ever died, what the state of our world would be, an outcome that wouldn't be good. What is a good age to die then? There is none, it is what it is. Some have a shorter journey than others and that's how it's meant to be. Is it acceptable when someone else's loved one dies but not when my loved one dies? Death has always had a presence in my life, it's as if there is a glass wall between death and me that creates separation. I know it's only a matter of time before the glass wall will not be there anymore. I accepted this awareness without feeling anxious, it is not so much about my own death. I imagine my loved one in flight, a soft, gentle movement, and so I am trying to take the sting out of death to soften my own losses.

We all want to live a life free of pain and suffering where nobody ever dies, that is what God had in mind all along. Life on earth is a journey to that place. The Bible doesn't teach that, but I like to think that Laurence and Duncan will be waiting for me, just over the horizon, to accompany me on my last journey, to the city of God. I am not afraid of crossing the bridge to the other side, I just hope the bridge is not on fire when I have to cross, but even so, Jesus will carry me through. (Isa 43:3 "When you walk through the fire, you will not be burned; the flame will not set you ablaze for I am the Lord your God"). I do whatever possible through exercise and a healthy lifestyle to avoid any unpleasant last days, but even so, if those days come, I will face them without regrets or guilty feelings.

Imagine...floating on air
drifting towards the clouds
Free at last...
of heavy burdens and sorrow

Looking down on earth
to living colors of ice and ocean
So breathtakingly beautiful
So incomplete with chill and turmoil
If the incomplete is so exquisite
how much more the complete?

Slowly moving further away
to where earth and heaven meet
And at last...the journey complete
to be released unto God
while I try to live with the loss

— *INCOMPLETE*

2 Cor 12:2 "I know a man in Christ who was caught up to the third heaven—He was caught up to paradise. He heard inexpressible things, things that man is not permitted to tell."

DESERT STORM

Without the desert storm, there will never be new life

I have lost many loved ones before they completed their lives, when they were way too young. I was not ready to be left by them, I feel their presence all around me. I want to touch their skin, see the smile on their lips that spreads to their eyes. I remember them often in many different ways, a voice I hear calling my name, the familiar footsteps coming through the door, the face I see in the shadows on the wall, and I yearn for that togetherness. Even though painful thoughts still cross my mind, they don't cut quite as deep or linger quite as long.

1 Co 15:54-56 "Death has been swallowed up in victory. Where, oh death is victory Where, oh death, is your sting. The sting of death is sin... (God) gives the victory through our Lord Jesus Christ."

Dark clouds are gathering
as angels watch in awe
and we brace for the storm
The wind howls a fright
as furious thunder strikes

We all watch in anticipation and fear
for the storm pouring over us is severe

And after forever it seemed
the sun begins to emerge as before
the winds and dark clouds leave
and there is thunder no more

With the light and the passing of the storm
emerges the jubilance of new life just born

Death and destruction passed
and everything became new at last
As angels watch in awe
God smiles down on His creation

— *RAIN IN THE SERENGETI*

Ps 77:17,18 "The clouds poured down water, the skies resounded with thunder, your arrow flashed back and forth. Your thunder was heard in the whirlwind. Your lightning lit up the world; the earth trembled and quaked."

Chapter Eleven

GRANDMA DAYS

Old age is a relative concept.

GRANDKIDS

As sure as death impacts our life, life continues in all its glory. The single pleasures of family and grandchildren remain to be embraced and often soothes the soul more than anything else can. Our plans for Markus's 8th birthday party were underway and as often is the case, I volunteered to make the cake. The request; a chocolate cake adorned with candy. I went to the store to pick up the ingredients and couldn't help but remember the clown cake I made for Angie and Jeanette and how Laurence and Duncan ate all the M&M's off the cake. The warm memory made me smile as I picked up candy for the cake and couldn't help but wonder if any of my grandchildren would attempt to sneak candy off this cake.

No-one is around
Not a movement or a sound
What could have happened
To the face of the clown

It didn't look like this before
I left and wasn't gone that long
Now I couldn't believe what I saw
Half the face was not there anymore

When I left the cake on the table
I didn't think my little boys were able
To pick off the candy to eat
The face of the clown that looked so neat

Now many years went by
I am standing here in the isle
To get candy so I can make

Yet another birthday cake

Remembering my two little boys
And how quickly they disappeared
When the face of the clown looked so weird
And they didn't want to come near it

People come and go as time goes by
But memories stay to bring us joy
Remembering my two little boys
I just shook my head and smiled

— FACE OF THE CLOWN

Ps 127:3 "Sons are a heritage from the Lord. Children a reward from Him."

TO AVERY

I began spending time with my great-granddaughter, Avery Belle Cronje, when she was 2.5-years old. Her initials are ABC and she knew the alphabet when she was still in diapers. At that age she could read short sentences without spelling out the words, she's equally good with numbers and can tell how many objects are on the table without counting them. Her ability to count makes her a good card player and we often play now that she's older, she told me her Papi taught her how to play.

Her favorite expression is "oh my goodness." She named the rooms in my house, like the toy room, or the music room, and likes to choose where she wants to play. She learned the love of music from her dad, Cameron, who is a talented musician. She will often ask to listen to Piano or Classical Guitar music and likes to call objects by their names. My gym bag became 'Ouma's diaper bag' and it's not uncommon for me to find some of her toys, that she shared with me, in my 'diaper bag'. I enjoy our time together so much. While visiting one day, she asked me how old I am, I told her that I'm very old, I'm seventy-one. She looked at me puzzled and then she said: "Yes Ouma, that is a big number." I find her ability to carry a conversation and her mature ways of communicating extraordinary. She has an intense way of making eye contact and to hold that contact, almost as if she is searching for a deeper understanding and truth.

You are wonderfully created
Unique beyond compare
There is no one else like you

Why do I love you so

I don't really know
You tip-toed into my heart
And start to touch forgotten emotions
You brought back part of me long gone

Little girl
Why do I love you so
I don't really know
I want to hold you close – always

But as time goes by
you might fade away into the past
Leaving me with memories hard to bear
but still, I'm glad they're there

–– LITTLE GIRL

Ps 139:14 "I praise You because I am fearfully and wonder-fully made; Your works are wonderful, I know that full well."

HEART GAMES

These are hard games indeed

> *If I must...*
> *who is there to trust*
> *What a world to live in*
> *Where shall I begin*
> *and where can I find*
> *a sincere and honest mind*
> *who doesn't delight in vain talk*
> *but straight and narrow few will walk*
> *and to find them – where shall I go?*
> *Will I live this life and not know?*
>
> — *HONESTY*

Ro 8:6 "For to be carnally minded is death but to be spiritually minded is life and peace."

Do not let a kiss fool you, and do not let a fool kiss you.
—*Motivational Quotes*

It's not a good idea to believe everything that your friends tell you. When you really like someone but all you get is one date, don't be disappointed, never compromise your standards and put your heart out there just to be played with. Men who threaten to leave, use emotional blackmail or deceit, are not worthy of your affection. You're building your foundation on sand and the hurt of rejection goes deep, especially if there's a child involved. Wizen up precious girl, don't give your power away, these power games have been around since the beginning of time.

2 Ti 3:6 "They are the kind who worm their way into homes and gain control over weak- willed woman, who are loaded down with sin."

Girls and guys do not think the same, they differ in very important matters. Guys find, they concur, and then want to move on. Girls find, they bond, and then want to settle down.

Abbreviated version of *"Sigh no more ladies"*, Shakespeare

> *Sigh no more ladies, sigh no more*
> *Men were deceivers ever*
> *One foot in sea and one foot on shore*
> *To one thing constant, never*
> *Then sigh not so, but let them go*
> *The fraud of men were ever so*
> *since summer first was leavy*
> *Then sigh not so but let them go*

LOCUSTS

Through my brokenness, I found understanding

Joel 2:25 "I will repay you for the years the locusts have eaten – the great locust and the young locust, the other locusts and the locust swarm."

As a 17-year old I made choices that devastated my life, now as a 71-year old the tables are definitely reversed as I can objectively look at situations and make decisions accordingly. What I like about being older is that I feel confident, I have more wisdom and much better understanding. It was a long hard journey to reach this contentment, there were times I didn't think I could survive all that came my way.

I don't regret my past even though sometimes my thoughts still go into overdrive, like those small wild monkeys back in Durban, jumping from one branch to the next. At times I don't know which way my mind will turn, either bringing back bad memories or thinking positively about the future. If I could go back in time to correct the wrongs, I wouldn't want to. If I did get another chance, I would make different mistakes that would take me to another place, where I might not want to be. I am where I need to be, even though it was a tiresome battle that brought me here.

The conscious thoughts I allow into my mind will eventually kick in, creating either good habits or not so good habits. I love poetry as it helps me to look at life with deeper understanding, considering various angles to approach problematic situations. As you've noticed, my poetry is peppered throughout the experiences of my life in this book, to expose the more poignant perspectives.

When I was young and carefree
Before the years had changed me
There was so much I didn't know
And it came to me, but oh, so slow
The stories of youth
Do not tell the truth
You know you are living lies
When life is full of heartaches
And goodbyes

At least by now I know
where I want to go
Do I miss youth?
To tell you the truth
I do not think so

--- DO I MISS YOUTH

Ps 25:7 "Remember not the sins of my youth and my rebellious ways;
according to your love remember me, for you are good, O Lord."

FEAR OF THE UNKNOWN

Ecc 5:3 "As a dream comes when there are too many cares."

> *Like bad dreams, repetitive themes*
> *about the past I barely survived*
> *come back to bring pain revived*
> *just as I begin to thrive*
>
> *but this time I know God*
>
> *Before I was a total wreck*
> *And was standing on the edge*
> *Of total self-destruction*
> *I didn't seek God's protection*
>
> *when I was without God*
>
> *Sometimes the devil gets his kicks*
> *To try the same old dirty tricks*
> *That work so well for him before*
> *But it cannot break me anymore*
>
> *because now I belong to God*
>
> *— IN MY LIFE*

1 Co 10:13 "No temptation has seized you except what is common to man. And God is faithful, He will not let you be tempted beyond what you can bear. But when you are tempted, He will also provide a way out so that you can stand under it."

. . .

I often wonder why life takes so much from me, but one thing I do know, God will never abandon me. He will circle the wagons like bringing a support group into my life ahead of time. These continuous tragedies are devastating and emotionally crippling and leaves me feeling vulnerable. I don't know what life might take from me in the future, but I know there will be a way through.

Even though I have made great progress recovering, I still experience some really bad days. The same trauma keeps revisiting me in many different variations. What lessons do I need to learn that will give me better understanding to deal with this? I can't say I am fearful of that which I can see, I'm more frightened of the boogieman and what is hiding in the unknown. I don't like to go out on my own, I anticipate disaster, getting lost in the unknown, and unable to find my way back to where I need to be. It's not about what I fear, the question is why do I still fear the unknown?

JUST BEING THERE

In the recesses of my mind
I find vivid memories
of long-gone times
when the nights were kind
and my daydreaming fine

But as the seasons change
time lets me feel and be
We live, we grow old – we die
And with the last kiss
the future turns into the past

— *THE LAST KISS*

Ps 146:4 "When his breath departs, he returns to the earth; on that very day his plans perish."

This is an excellent description of old age: Ecclesiastes 12:1-7 (from a Bible Study)

"Remember your Creator in the days of your youth, before the days of trouble come and the years approach when you will say, "I find no plea-sure in them;" Before the sun and the light and the moon and the stars grow dark, (poor eyesight) and the clouds return after the rain. When the keepers of the house tremble (trembling hands) and the strong man stoop (unsteady legs) when the grinders cease because they are few (difficulty chewing) and those looking through the windows grow dim; (weak eyes).

"When the doors to the street are close (hard of hearing) and the sound of grinding fades; when men rise up at the sound of birds but all their songs grow faint. When men are afraid of heights and of dangers in the street (fear of falling) when the almond tree blossoms and the grasshopper drags himself along and desire no longer is stirred (lost interest). Then man goes to his eternal home (he dies) and the mourners go about the street (funeral).

"Remember him (God) before the silver cord is severed or the golden bowl is broken; before the pitcher is shattered at the spring, or the wheel broken at the well (before dying). The dust returns to the ground it came from, and the spirit returns to God who gave it. And so the future turns into the past."

WHERE EARTH AND HEAVEN MEET

You find Paradise

> *There is a place*
> *where earth and heaven meet*
> *and brokenness are made complete*
>
> *There is a place not far from here*
> *where loved ones I held dear*
> *will once again be near*
>
> *There is a place where I will go*
> *but when – is not for me to know*
>
> *— THERE IS A PLACE*

Ac 7:55 "(he) looked up to heaven and saw the glory of God, and Jesus standing at the right hand of God. "Look" he said, "I see heaven open and the Son of Man standing at the right hand of God."

1 Th 4:13 "Brothers we don't want you to be ignorant about those who fall asleep or to grieve like the rest of men, who have no hope."

Rev 2:7 "To him who overcomes, I will give the right to eat from the tree of life, which is in the paradise of God."

. . .

Rev 21:4 "He will wipe every tear from their eyes. There will be no more death or mourning or crying or pain, for the old order of things has passed away."

Lk 23:42 "Then he said, "Jesus, remember me when you come into your kingdom. Jesus answered him, "I tell you the truth, today you will be with Me in paradise.""

2 Co 12:2 "I know a man in Christ – who was caught up to the third heaven. I know that this man, whether in the body or apart from the body I do not know – was caught up to paradise. He heard inexpressible things; things that man is not permitted to tell."

2 Ti 4:18 "The Lord will rescue me from every evil attack and will bring me safely to his heavenly kingdom."

Rev 19:11 "I saw heaven standing open and there before me was a white horse, whose rider is called Faithful and True. With justice He judges and makes war. "

EPILOGUE

Horsemen of the Apocalypse

The Covid-19 pandemic reminds me of a time long ago, when my two sets of identical twins were pre-teens. When some mischief happened, it was practically impossible to find out from eyewitnesses who the guilty party was. The solution was to send all four of them to the bedroom to go and think. The rule was that no one was allowed to go anywhere, until the guilty one confessed, once that was concluded we could take it from there.

Sometimes I wonder if God has put the whole world in time-out to go think things through. During the height of the pandemic, just about everybody had to stay home and until the crisis had resolved, nobody was going to continue with their life as usual. Yet while people had to stay home, the air became cleaner, the water cleared, and animals came out of hiding.

The simple truth, the earth is dying.

Watchmen shout the warning
about a time of mourning
a time to pray
Four horsemen are on the way

The rider on a white horse
carries a bow but no arrow
and brings promises of peace

but it is not so – behind him follows….

The rider on a red horse, who carries a big sword.
He has power to take peace from earth
and make men slay each other.

The rider on a black horse

who carries a pair of scales, brings famine
"a quart of wheat for a day's wages"

The rider on a pale horse
has power over a fourth of the earth
to kill by sword, famine, and plagues

we look, but don't see
we hear, but don't listen

— *HORSEMEN OF THE*
APOCALYPSE

(Ecc 12:1) "Remember your Creator in the days of your youth, before the day of trouble come and the years approach when you will say, I find no pleasure in them."

(Mt 25:13) "Therefore, keep watch, because you do not know the day or the hour."

(Mt 24:36) "No-one knows about that day or hour, not even the angels in heaven, nor the Son, but only the Father."

(Mt 24:32) "Now learn this lesson from the fig-tree: As soon as its twigs get tender and its leaves come out, you know that summer is near. Even so, when you see all these things, you know that (the time) is near, right at the door."

.   .   .

(Mt 24:29, 30) "The sun will be darkened, and the moon will not give its light; the stars will fall from the sky and the heavenly bodies will be shaken. At that time the sign of the Son of Man will appear in the sky, and all the nations of the earth will mourn. They will see the Son of Man coming on the clouds of the sky, with power and great glory."

(2 Pe 3:10) "But the day of the Lord will come like a thief. The heavens will disappear with a roar; the elements will be destroyed by fire, and the earth and everything in it will be laid bare. Since everything will be destroyed in this way."

(Rev 6:12, 13, 14) "There was a great earthquake. The sun turned black...the whole moon turned blood red, and the stars in the sky fell to earth...The sky receded like a scroll, rolling up, and every mountain and island was removed from its place."

(Isa 13:13) "Therefore, I will make the heavens tremble; and the earth will shake from its place, at the wrath of the Lord Almighty, in the day of His burning anger."

(2 Pe 3:12) "That day will bring about the destruction of the heavens by fire, and the elements will melt in the heat."

TIMELINE

Significant Losses

The years teach much which the days never knew
—Anonymous

[1953] Uncle's friend drowned, I couldn't remember but I couldn't forget either.

[1956] Paternal grandfather died from Diabetes, those last snap-shots never fade away.

[1958] Childhood friend Linda died from Diphtheria, reality of the empty window.

[1964] My sister Annelize died after her lungs failed from Cerebral palsy, ignorance is bliss.

[1966] My cousin Henning's stillborn baby, journey not yet taken, I didn't understand.

[1967] My family members by marriage, Eugene (3-months) and Freddy (6-years old) died in a house fire.

[1970] My divorce and subsequent breakdown, no-one ever gets broken beyond recovery, God can fix it.

[1972] Paternal grandmother died from Lung cancer, amazing common sense with relationships.

[1974] My baby Jacob miscarried, now I understand the depth of that pain.

[1982] My sister miscarried her only baby and became a second Mom to my kids.

[1984] Maternal grandmother died from a heart attack, never overstayed her welcome.

[1987] Emigrated to USA, gone are all those familiar roads that lead to familiar places.

[1989] My cousin Henning died in a car crash, harsh reality of losing my homeland and my people.

[1989] My father-in-law, Ron, died in a car crash, unconditional love.

[1991 April] My brother Lourens died by suicide, the significance of childhood adjustments.

[1991 April] My son Laurence is murdered, his longing for family togetherness.

[1991 May] My aunt Miem died from Jaundice, my second Mom, absolute loyalty.

[1991 November] My uncle Dawie died from a heart attack, strong but gentle desert person, he had freedom.

[1992] Hurricane Andrew hit our home, pictured the desolation I felt inside of me.

[1996] My father-in-law, Daan, died from kidney failure, my dad's soul mate, two of a kind.

[1998 June] My father died from Pneumonia, honesty, he did what was right no matter how difficult.

[1998 June] My uncle Visser robbed and murdered, respected in the community, loved by children.

[1999 February] My mother-in-law died from strokes, spiritual mother, total acceptance of me from the start.

[1999 June] My mother died from a heart attack, best mom she could be, in spite of her poor health.

[1999 November] My aunt Maggie died from suicide, I made peace with her decision, I could understand why.

[2010 April] My step granddaughter, Lindsay, died from Cancer, her strong desire to live.

[2010 August] My son-in-law, Randy, died in a car crash, the respect he showed.

[2010 October] My son Duncan, died in a car crash, just to love and be loved.

[2012] My cousin Bennie, robbed and murdered, loved the farm even though it was dangerous.

[2013] My friend, Sam, died from a heart attack, he spoke my language and emigrated with us.

[2014] My friend, Julie, died from Cancer, she showed many how to die with dignity.

[2015] Bettye, Randy's Mom, died from Cancer, courage that came from her peace of mind.

[2016 April] My sister Elina is murdered, lost consciousness with a prayer on her lips.

[2016 August] My friend, Liz, dies from Lupus, I admire her courage, never complained, and always encouraged.

ABOUT THE AUTHOR

Elizabeth Kidson is a South African born poet and author. This is her first publication, a blend of autobiography and poetry.

Elizabeth was born in Vryburg, South Africa, in 1949 and grew up in an Afrikaans home as the daughter of Lourens and Anna Vorster. Her first marriage ended after much unhappiness but blessed her with a son (Marius) and a daughter (Anita). Her second marriage gave her a set of twin boys (Laurence & Duncan) as well as a set of twin girls (Angela & Jeanette).

While pursuing the proud trade of homemaker for well over a decade, she also indulged her other passions of floristry, growing orchids, stained glass art, and cake decorating, thus toiling as a handmaiden of the arts.

Her family emigrated to the United States of America during 1987 where they became citizens and continue to live today in Miami, Florida. What started out as a grand adventure full of promise in a new country, would bring its own tragedy.

Made in United States
Orlando, FL
18 May 2022

17989647R00133